Road test 1948 Series B Rapides waiting to be despatched (Ted Davis).

WORLD MOTOR CYCLES

VINCENT-HRD

Peter Carrick

 Patrick Stephens, Cambridge

First published in 1982

British Library Cataloguing in Publication Data

Carrick, Peter
   Vincent HRD. - (World motorcycles)
   1. Vincent HRD motorcycle - History
   I. Title   II. Series
   629.2'275   TL448.V/

ISBN 0-85059-512-6

Photoset in 10 pt Baskerville by Manuset Limited, Baldock, Herts. Printed in Great Britain on 100 gsm Fineblade coated cartridge, and bound, by The Garden City Press, Letchworth, Herts, for the publishers, Patrick Stephens Limited, Bar Hill, Cambridge, CB3 8EL, England.

Contents

Author's preface

Surely no more appropriate choice could have been made with which to begin this series of *World Motor Cycles*. Created by uncompromising idealists whose vision all too often conflicted with practical and commercial considerations, Vincent motor cycles have always embodied a very special kind of magic for a vast number of motor cycle enthusiasts. They continue to be remembered with deep affection, more than 25 years after the closure of the famous Stevenage works.

Those famous, classic machines of superior specification and exceptional performance were true 'knights of the road', and, as Tony Rose observes in Chapter 4, they significantly anticipated the super-bike era of the 1970s and '80s.

The Vincent story is complex and varied, at different times gloriously stimulating and pathetically depressing. In this new account I have tried to capture the atmosphere and movement of Vincent's significant days and put all the major factors together in what I hope will be generally accepted as a 'good read', with perhaps a somewhat different angle here and there on Vincent's indelible contribution to motor cycle history.

I wish to thank Cliff Brown for talking to me at length about Vincent, the factory, machines and events, and for making many of his personal files and notes available to me. I am also grateful to Jack Lazenby for information concerning the Picador project, particularly to Roy Harper and Ted Davis, to Glenn Dimmock, and to Tony Rose and A.C.F. Warner, the latter of Filtrate Ltd, for their help. I am particularly indebted to Mick Woollett and *Motor Cycle Weekly* for allowing me access to so many historical photographs and to others (as acknowledged) who have provided photographs.

Peter Carrick

Vincent and the HRD inheritance

There was nothing exceptional in 1928 in Philip C. Vincent wanting to design, build and sell motor cycles. The industry had been founded on the basis of inventive individuals applying their own ideas and assembling machines themselves. Factories like Norton, Velocette and Rudge, though solidly established and rapidly building an international reputation for British designs and technical excellence—mainly through the impetus of racing on the Isle of Man and at Brooklands—were still not sufficiently awe-inspiring to frighten off the young and ambitious. So Philip Vincent was by no means alone amongst young motor cycle enthusiasts wanting to put their own ideas into practice. He was youthful, talented and intelligent, and his studies in Mechanical Sciences at King's College, Cambridge, fitted him for the career he saw for himself as the head of his own motor cycle manufacturing company.

Some years earlier, during his public schooldays at Harrow, he had become interested in motor cycles. Passionately enthusiastic by 1924, he bought his first machine, a 350 cc sidevalve BSA. Riding this and subsequent models highlighted what were, to his enquiring mind, some fairly plain errors in both design and manufacture and three years later, after he had moved on to Cambridge, he seized the chance to build his first motor cycle.

The crusade had begun while he was still at Harrow. He owned at one time a 398 cc ABC machine with a basic system of rear springing. Vincent soon realised its limitations, but was fully convinced, because of the extra comfort he enjoyed while riding, of the desirability of rear springing. He worked out a design for what he considered to be a much improved frame which included rear springing, but not until he got to Cambridge did he have the chance to work on the idea. After introducing a number of minor modifications, he looked towards producing his prototype motor cycle.

Vincent's father was a prosperous cattle farmer in the Argentine and he responded favourably when his son asked him for money to build his prototype machine. By no means a true thoroughbred by comparison with Vincent models which were to

Highly representative of the Vincent-HRD dynasty. This Series A Rapide was sold for £128 in 1938 as the fastest production machine on two, three or four wheels (Ted Davis).

follow, this first machine was nonetheless very capable, if somewhat robust. Top speed was in excess of 80 mph and it gave the energetic Philip Vincent around 10,000 miles of comfortable, troublefree travel. Encouraged, he persuaded his father to make a further investment in his ideas, Vincent senior only agreeing, however, after he had received a favourable on-the-spot report from Frank Walker, an engineering colleague and a knowledgeable motor cyclist. Premises at Stevenage in Hertfordshire, empty when viewed but previously used as a brewery and, much earlier, by a firm of carriage-builders, were taken over and Philip Vincent's father put Walker in as the new firm's managing director.

It was 1928 and having been advised that the best way to begin business was to buy an existing name, Vincent found that Omega and HRD were on offer. The latter concern, started in 1924 by Howard Davies, a TT winner on his own 500 cc machine a year later, had made its mark before falling on hard times. The firm had subsequently been acquired, following voluntary liquidation, by Ernie Humphries of the OK Supreme factory. Davies had been Philip Vincent's idol as the latter's passion for motor cycles developed. Once he knew he could acquire the HRD name and goodwill, plus some stock, jigs and tools—as well as the original drawings, for just

£400, he looked no further. So in 1928 Philip Vincent travelled to Wolverhampton to buy the remnants of HRD, signed the documents, and the Vincent-HRD Company Ltd was soon established.

Howard Davies' HRD models had been admired for their advanced design—and he for his 'quality first' philosophy—and although all components were 'bought in', his ideas had a bearing on future motor cycle trends. He was, for instance, one of the first manufacturers to use a saddle tank. Davies' challenging attitude was akin to that of Vincent, who was intent on producing machines of high quality which did not automatically follow the accepted pattern. By early 1930 he had two newly-designed machines completed, both incorporating his favoured triangulated rear sprung frame.

From the outset Vincent had been totally committed to the concept of rear wheel springing. His experimental spring frame of 1927 incorporated a partly welded and partly brazed rear fork and rigid main bearing cross member, consisting of two large-diameter short sections made of heavy gauge $2\frac{1}{4}$ in diameter tube. This formed the basis of his triangulated production frame introduced in 1928. Much neater, it was mainly of welded construction. There was such a hardened prejudice against spring frames at the time—on the grounds of safety and because some very indifferent types were then being

Part of the famous Number 1 factory in High Street, Stevenage, occupied from 1932 to 1957. (Cliff Brown).

made—that Vincent found it necessary at first to show his new spring frames looking as much like ordinary rigid frames as possible. Fitted with JAP standard double-port overhead valve engines, one of the prototypes became a 350, the other a 250 cc racer with a nickel-plated frame. Testing Vincent's ideas on one of his early machines at the famous Brooklands circuit, racer Brian Twist came a creditable sixth in the 200-mile race at an average of 67.58 mph.

The young company looked ahead to the annual Motor Cycle Show at Olympia, London, but had difficulty in getting supplies through on time for the five models intended for exhibition. After a massive effort the deadlines were met and the first Vincent-HRD machines to be 'shown' were unveiled. The spring frame had been modified with telescopic housings fitted with integral adjustable dampers. All five machines had JAP engines—three 500s (one racing), a 600 and a 350. Black enamel was chosen as the standard finish and although the famous HRD tank transfers were retained, they were included as part of an overall 'logo' which incorporated the new Vincent scroll.

Alas, not one order was taken at the show and the first 12 months were lean indeed for the new company, fewer than 25 machines being sold. All round, times were hard. Britain's General Strike of 1926 had been followed by the Wall Street crash three years later. Many manufacturers were to go out of business and Philip Vincent's precious enterprise tottered on the verge of collapse when much needed cash support promised by his father was frozen in Argentina when that country imposed general restrictions on the movement of capital there. Salvation came when Captain G. Clarke, of the Imperial Tobacco Company and a keen motor cyclist, was persuaded to invest in Vincent's ailing firm after his son, Bill, had been extremely impressed by a Vincent machine which he had bought. Captain Clarke then became chairman of Vincent-HRD and his son, Bill Clarke, joined the board.

For some time the firm continued to use JAP proprietary engines, but with lessening enthusiasm. A number of big-end seizures during road testing only accelerated Philip Vincent's determination to use an alternative engine and, in 1930, following Rudge's Senior and Junior victories on the Isle of Man, a Vincent with a Rudge Ulster 'Python' engine was offered for the first time.

Despite difficult trading conditions, Philip Vincent maintained his enthusiasm and energies. Modifications to his design included primary chain-covers for longer life, a longer and better looking tank, improved riding position, a more handsome overall appearance, and a better method of mounting the engine and gearbox. There was also to be a new silencing system. The range in 1929 and '30 included models fitted with 498 cc and 600 cc racing JAP engines, 490 cc and 600 cc tourers, a super sports with a 490 cc JAP special, and a 350 cc model intended as a grass-track machine. This was never a success, despite Vincent's persistence, and was dropped after only about 18 months. Other improvements about this time were a spring-up prop stand, rear chain oiler, foot change as standard fitting, and three- or four-speed Burman gearboxes.

Overall the small firm made steady if unspectacular progress. In the first 12 months only 24 machines were sold, 36 during the 1930 season and then came a surge resulting in 60 orders being received between the Motor Cycle Shows of 1930 and '31. In the meantime Vincent's controversial spring frame had been widely talked about and acquired as many supporters as critics, certainly after a tough test by *The Motor Cycle* praised it. The factory was gradually building a solid reputation for hand-built motor cycles of both quality and performance. Even so, the economic slump affected business. The 1932 sales figures were down to just 55 and prices had to be reduced to encourage trade. Among a number of innovations in 1933 was a pivoted pillion seat which allowed a passenger to be carried without the rear frame springs having to be changed. For a time this was also a feature of New Imperial models, which in 1935 Vincents were to sell, along with their own models, direct to the public in an effort to boost business.

It was also about 1933 that the factory began to make more of its own components, this policy leading to the introduction of Vincent's unique dual braking system. There was more inclination now to use Rudge engines instead of JAP, though Vincent was persuaded for commercial reasons to use the latter when he took his machines to the Isle of Man for the TT Races for the first time in 1934. The result was disastrous. The promised engines arrived much later than anticipated, leaving the Vincent team of Jack Williams, Arthur Tyler and John Carr little time for proper practice, and numerous breakdowns before the race meant frantic telephone calls for replacement parts. When it seemed that the problem had been finally overcome and the bikes were recording encouraging times in practice, the JAP advisers threw the Vincent camp into further turmoil by recommending the fitting of new cam followers and Vincent's small contingent, already exhausted, were called into emergency action once more.

It was all in vain. All three bikes retired during

racing with mechanical problems and Philip Vincent was left bitter and angry from a sorry and costly experience. Phil Irving, the talented and far-sighted Australian engineer who had joined Vincents in the latter part of 1932 (and would help to produce Vincent's own engine), was present on the Island and the JAP failure again emphasised the factory's determination to push ahead quickly with work on their own engine. It is interesting to note that a Blackburne-powered Vincent had been raced in the Junior Manx Grand Prix in 1933 and that 500 cc JAP and Rudge engines and a Villiers 250 cc water-cooled two-stroke unit, which was available on special order, were used by Vincents in 1934.

Philip Vincent was by now known as PCV to distinguish him from Phil Irving. The two made a formidable combination, but were always destined to struggle within a kind of Jekyll and Hyde existence—trying to temper their natural creativity and idealism with the commercial requirements of the motor cycle buying public.

For 1935 Vincent-HRD concentrated on 500 cc and 600 cc machines, putting five different models on the market, the most interesting feature being the compact 498 cc Vincent-made engine designed for the factory by Phil Irving. It had a bore and stroke of 84 mm by 90 mm and all moving parts, with the exception of the valve springs, were enclosed. The cylinder head had a 16 degrees down-draught carburettor and single port exhaust. Integrally cast rocker boxes were fitted with detachable ribbed aluminium cover plates, the rockers being of the straight type as common on ohc engines and operated by two short push-rods set at an angle of as much as 62 degrees apart. Lubrication on the dry-sump principle was used with a double gear pump, and oil was fed under pressure direct to the big-end, timing-gear bearings and rockers.

Altogether it was an extremely interesting unit, designed for long life and ease of maintenance. The Vincent engine was fitted to three machines, the standard model, the sports bike and the TT special, the sports and TT models having aluminium-bronze heads. Prices, in that order, were £79-10s, £86 and £95. For the extra money the TT version had a specially tuned engine fitted and a racing magneto. It also had Duralumin mudguards and stays, straight-through exhaust pipe, close-ratio gears and a patent spring carrier. There was also a JAP-powered Vincent for 1935 at £75, and a 600 cc version with a two-port JAP engine at £76. All Vincent machines by this time were fitted with the unique duo-brake system featuring two-brake drums on each wheel, the rear pair being operated by rods.

The depressed 1930s savaged firms' natural ambitions and Philip Vincent fought a constant battle to find buyers for a quality product as individual and specialised as his Vincent-HRD motor cycles. A number of models which he introduced with pride and optimism were all too soon withdrawn, and as sales in Britain of motor cycles fell alarmingly by as much as 75 per cent, only his will to survive and his willingness to bend to market requirements kept the Stevenage factory going at all.

To broaden the appeal of his main models he had given them a more conventional appearance with a new diamond frame in place of the triangulated frame, tried for a toe-hold in the lighter machine market with a new Model L, which was powered by a 250 cc two-stroke Villiers engine, and he even moved outside strict motor cycle production with the Bantam three-wheeler delivery vehicle. No sales bonanza was expected from these measures, the objective being to keep things nudging along and, if possible, to encourage a slight edging-up of sales.

The three-wheeler differed basically from competitive models by having the third wheel positioned at the rear instead of the front, but although two versions were introduced, only about 30 Bantams in all were made. Philip Vincent regarded it as a capable model and certainly one of the best available at that time. The Model L light-weight machine became the Model W a year later. Overheating problems on the earlier version were overcome and although the machine was capable of more than 60 mph and could be driven hard all day without trouble, there were few takers for a hand-built machine at a higher price when cheaper, admittedly inferior rigid-framed bikes were on sale elsewhere. The machine was discontinued in 1935.

It was immediately after returning from the TT débâcle in 1934 that work had begun earnestly on the design of Vincent's own engine. The objective was to have it ready for the annual motor show, four months hence, and Phil Irving did much of the work, Vincent relying heavily on his mechanical talent and his remarkable knowledge of competitors' engines. The work was finished in October. The Vincent power units were to be known as the Meteor in standard form, the Comet when built into a sports machine, and the TT Replica when produced as a racer. The engine was basically an upright single-cylinder ohv 500 with unique double valve guides (giving a much slower rate of wear) and high camshaft location. The oil pump was gear driven and easy to maintain.

The prototypes needed very little alteration and all three models performed well, the Comet's top speed being well in excess of 90 mph. Handling was good and so was the braking system. The bikes soon made an impact with performance machine enthusiasts and it was this encouraging reception which led Philip Vincent into the production of a 1,000 cc V-twin.

By 1935 Philip Vincent might have been forgiven for thinking that the worst of the bad trading times were behind him. That year his firm sold 130 machines, compared with 36 five years earlier. A return to the Isle of Man with a modified engine which cured the worrying tendency of the earlier engine to fill its crankcase with oil, and a promising seventh position by Jack Williams in the Senior race, enhanced Vincent's reputation. By 1936 the use of proprietary engines had ended, all five 'show' models for that year featuring the factory's own engine in various states of tune.

The presence of Vincent machinery on the Isle of Man and at Brooklands was building a reputation for the factory among riders who wanted faster machines, and it was to meet this growing demand that the 1,000 cc V-twin was introduced. There were few big V-twins about in 1936, so when the brand new 998 cc Vincent Rapide was unveiled at London's Motor Cycle Show that year, it was a sensation. Two of the factory's own single-cylinder, high-camshaft engines had been set in a 47-degree V, mounted on a massive crankcase and sandwiched into an economical-sized frame, together with twin carburettors, magnetos and two-speed gearbox. The unit had light alloy cylinders with steel liners and hairpin valve springs. The frame was of the single down-tube cradle type, with pivoted triangle type rear springing and girder forks with friction dampers. It was capable of 110 mph, yet its weight was only 22 lb (10 kg) more than the Vincent 500 from which it had been derived.

By this time George Brown had been taken on by Vincent and his brother Clifford was also working there as assistant development engineer. He and Bill Ling built the TT Replica engines used in the Comet Special Vincents, and when called upon by Philip Vincent and Phil Irving to make the first 1,000 cc twin they called it the plumber's nightmare because there were so many pipes all over it. But in spite of its initial shortcomings the Rapide, as the machine had been christened, showed enough promise to suggest to Vincent that effort should be made to produce improved versions. Post-war developments of the big machine were to build a solid reputation for the factory and secure for Vincent an honoured place in motor cycle history. Compared with the reputation of the 1,000 cc Vincents in the late 1940s and early 1950s, the pre-war Vincents were really nothing very special. They were comfortable enough to ride, steered well and showed a good turn of speed, but on the big

machines, the transmission was suspect and, not being strong enough, often caused trouble. Philip Vincent, while acknowledging that the clutch on the Rapide developed a poor reputation over the years, felt that the criticism was in part unjustified and that it suffered in public opinion largely because of its unconventional design. But there is no doubt that the original design of the clutch incorporated a basic error and this fault was never totally eradicated until its production ended in 1955.

Instead of classifying the production batches in years, as was then customary, Vincent decided to group their machines in Series form, these first pre-war Rapides being designated Series A. Altogether, 78 Series A Rapides were built between 1936 and 1939 and at the same time the factory continued to make the increasingly popular Comet and Meteor, though the Comet Special was withdrawn in 1938, this market by then being satisfied by the Series A Rapide.

Two significant individual performances on Vincent machinery in the late 1930s belong to George Brown and Stanley 'Ginger' Wood. George rode a Series A model over a kilometre at Brooklands at an impressive speed approaching 113 mph and Wood (then Vincent's chief tester) on a similar machine, set a new petrol-benzole lap record at Donington. George was to go on to even greater deeds on Vincent-powered machinery after the war; Wood's truly epic ride was at a Bank Holiday meeting in 1938. Philip Vincent wanted to use the race as a showcase to give the public an idea of what a super-sports roadster could do when it was a product of the Vincent factory. There were a few catcalls when Wood was left on the line as he struggled to push-start, but once away he was determined to show what he, and the Vincent, could do. He amazed the crowd by overtaking some riders on the very first lap, even though he had started late, and the bike sped round Donington at about 130 mph, faster than any bike had been previously raced there. His leap over Starkeys looked terrifying as the machine took off over the brow and landed about 100 ft down the hill. It was a galvanising performance and although the clutch failed before the end, Philip Vincent was well satisfied that the purpose of the exercise had been well and truly achieved.

A lot of the ground work on the new breed of Vincent big-twins was done during the latter part of the war, though they did not emerge (as the Series B Rapides) until late September 1946. And George Brown and Ginger Wood's racing successes were the prelude to some remarkable performances by the big Vincent in the years immediately following the war.

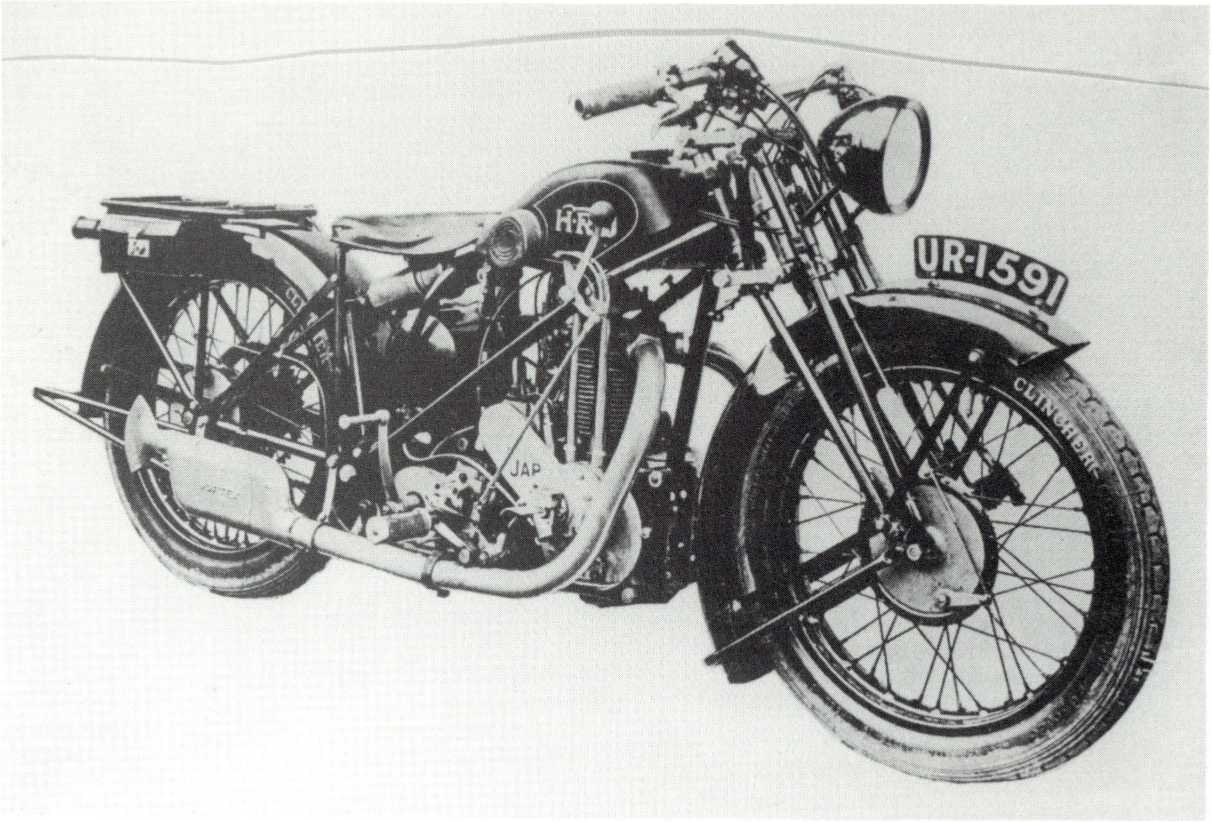
H·R·D
UR·1591
JAP
CLINCHER

H·R·D
JAP

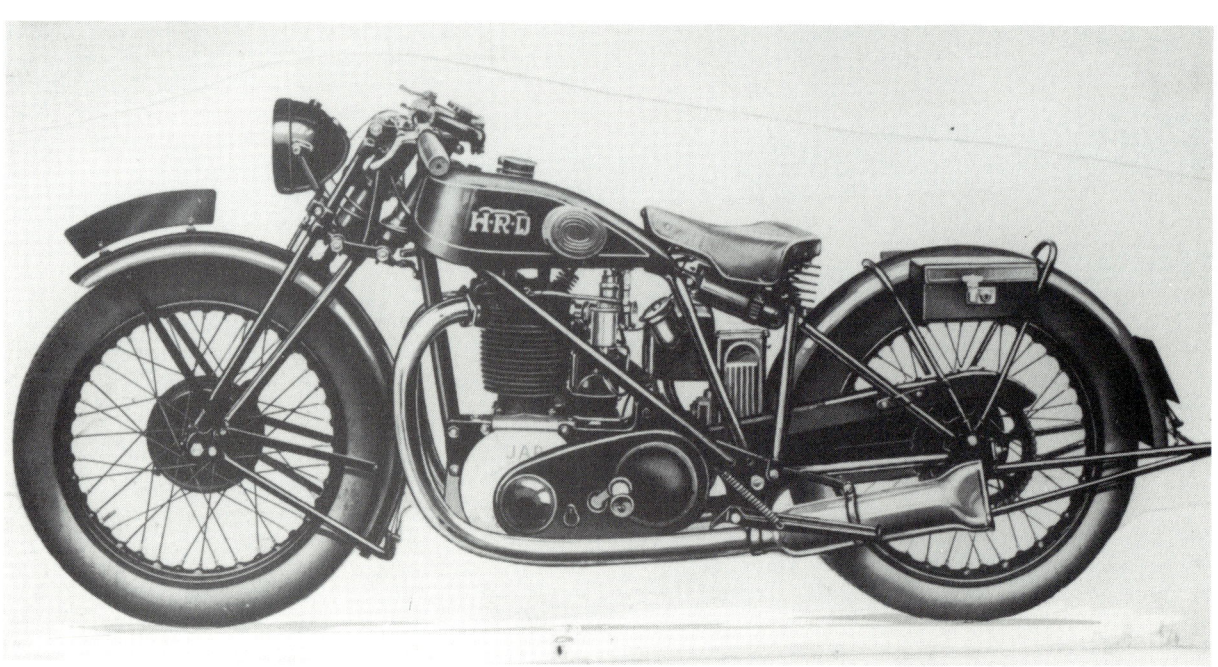

Left *An early Model B JAP-powered Vincent-HRD of 1928. Note the rear spring frame (Ted Davis).*

J.A.P. Models

500 c.c.; and 600 c.c. O.H.V. Models.

Below left *The 1931 500 cc Vincent sports with spring frame, sold for £68-10s. (Motor Cycle Weekly).*

The Vincent H.R.D. "Comet"

The 500 c.c. "Comet."

Top right *The model J Vincent fitted with a JAP engine (Cliff Brown).*

Above right *The 500 cc Comet of 1935 (Cliff Brown).*

The Vincent H.R.D. "Meteor"

The 500 c.c. "Meteor."

Right *The 500 cc Meteor of 1935, a slightly detuned version of the Comet (Cliff Brown).*

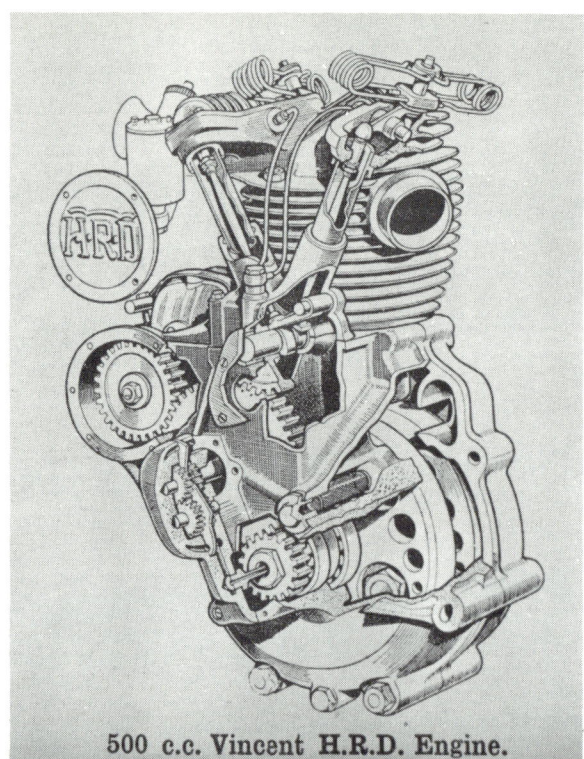

500 c.c. Vincent H.R.D. Engine.

Far left *The 500 cc Vincent-HRD engine of 1936—the first full Vincent-manufactured engine* (Cliff Brown).

Left *In the days of promise. An early company advertisement* (Cliff Brown).

Below left *A 1934 Vincent-HRD Model W, powered by a 250 cc Villiers water-cooled engine* (Motor Cycle Weekly).

Top right *The 1935 Comet, capable of 100 mph to standard specification* (Motor Cycle Weekly).

Above right *Vincent-HRD—1935 style* (Motor Cycle Weekly).

Right *The Series A Vincent-HRD* (Motor Cycle Weekly).

Above *The Series A Vincent twin . . . dismantled* (Motor Cycle Weekly).

Left *The new 1936 standard 500 cc Comet engine* (Motor Cycle Weekly).

Right *A 1936 Supercharged Series A ready for the TT* (Motor Cycle Weekly).

Above right *Christened the 'plumber's nightmare' by the backroom boys, this is the early version of the Series A Rapide twin, made from 1936 to the outbreak of war in 1939* (Motor Cycle Weekly).

Above *Ginger Wood on the works 998 cc Series A racer in 1938—the bike which held the 1,000 cc lap record at Donington that same year* (Ted Davis).

Below *George Brown racing the Cadwell Special* (Cliff Brown).

Above *Standard 1938 Series A Comet road bike, 500 cc and costing approximately £90 when new (Motor Cycle Weekly).*
Below *Close up of the Vincent-HRD of 1938, showing primary drive. Note the duplex chain, unusual for those days but in common use now (Motor Cycle Weekly).*

The war years

In 1938 there were few who felt deep in their hearts that some kind of European conflict could be averted, in spite of British Premier Neville Chamberlain's post-Munich assurances. 'Peace in our time' seemed out of character with reality as war preparations throughout the land gathered momentum and motor cycle sales slumped. While the larger companies like BSA would soon be working round the clock making motor cycles and motor cycle combinations for the Army, Vincent's factory was neither large enough nor sufficiently mechanised to warrant continued motor cycle production as part of the war effort.

However, there was to be a useful war-time role for Vincents nonetheless, the founder keeping his firm together with sub-contract work making parts for Naval shells and, later, with a direct Ministry of Supply contract manufacturing casings for land mines. By 1940 the factory was producing components for the RAF, like landing lamps and rocket fuzes for Wellington bombers and Mosquito fighter bombers. The machine shop capacity was doubled, new plant installed, and the factory worked day and night. The declaration of war on September 3 1939, had brought a final switch from making motor cycles to war production and although Philip Vincent was to be actively working out his post-war plans for motor cycle production during the later stages of the war, Vincent motor cycle production ceased totally for six years.

In the meantime Bill Clarke, whose enthusiasm and admiration for the Vincent concept had brought his father's life-saving investment into Vincents at a crucial time in the early days, joined the RAF and the factory mourned the loss when, on one of the famous 1,000-bomber raids over Germany, Squadron Leader Clarke was shot down and killed.

War-time also brought Philip Vincent the opportunity to develop his ideas for a new motor cycle engine. The spur was the chance of an important Air Ministry contract. What emerged was a 500 cc version of an opposed piston charged two-stroke marine engine giving 15 bhp at 3,000 rpm, with greater cruising fuel economy than that provided by an ohv four-stroke, easy starting in all conditions, and reliability.

Since the new engine would be required to power a new long-distance lifeboat, it had to be capable of running at an equivalent 70 mph at nearly 70 mpg for months, and to be efficient when fuelled by 73 octane pool petrol at the one extreme, or high-

The Picador experimental target aircraft on the launching pad in North Africa in 1953. Vincent were responsible for the engine, (Cliff Brown).

leaded 100 octane aviation spirit at the other. The Air Ministry saw an application for these new large lifeboats mainly in the Pacific, travelling long-distance to pick up air crews who had come down in the sea. This marine engine was even at this time considered by Phil Irving and Philip Vincent as having an application in a production motor cycle after the war ended.

Phil Irving and Matt Wright worked on the engine's development and a new sound-proof test house was built with all the most modern equipment so that the engines could be run continuously without outside noise. Irving and Wright built the first marine engine and Cliff Brown was the chief AID inspector. Vincent, himself, found the twin crank arrangement was a possible way of providing independent timing for the transfer and the exhaust ports in relation to each other, and the uniflow scavenge was a great advantage, especially when coupled with the positive pressure feed of the charge gases into the firing cylinders from the positive displacement charging cylinders.

The exhaust crankshaft was timed 24 degrees ahead of the transfer crankshaft and the subsequent timing relationships ensured that none of the fresh charge was wasted. It was accepted as a very good design and was also oil-proof. The engine was so smooth that Cliff Brown, who witnessed the tests, said that it was possible to put an eight-sided threepenny piece on the engine and it would not move.

The first engine test was started on May 27 1944, and ended its development contract on January 31 1945. After being stopped and stripped down for AID inspection it was restarted on February 1 1945, ending its type test on March 8 of the same year. The second engine was started on February 23 1945, and ended its test on July 2, followed by the acceptance test. Altogether the two engines had been run for 802 hours and 32 minutes, and Cliff Brown said he knew of no other engines which had been run for so long with efficiency. Unfortunately changes in the specification delayed final acceptance until after the war, but Vincents did build a small batch of 50 engines for delivery later that decade. That, then, was the end of it, for advances made with helicopters for air-sea rescue work meant there was no possibility of further orders.

Vincent and Irving later seriously considered using the marine engine for two possible post-war projects—a high-performance production motor cycle and a small family car. Both were rejected, the first on the grounds of high production costs and the second—after impressive tests and after Vincent had patented the idea—because the firm had depended on substantial orders for the marine

engine coming from the Air Ministry to get the unit cost down to a realistic level for use in the car. But as already noted, the engine orders were never forthcoming and the project was abandoned, but not before the prototype body and chassis had been built. This unique unfinished car—perhaps the forerunner of the historic Mini—was left to gather dust and cobwebs in the rafters of the Stevenage works, before being dragged out and chopped up for firewood.

Before the war ended Vincents were contracted to design a number of engines required for the driving of signalling generators, but a possible larger version of the marine engine, following an approach from the Air Ministry, never came to anything.

Though not strictly 'Vincent in battledress', since it was after the war that work was first started on the project, any mention of the factory's non-motor cycle production must include the Picador target aircraft engine. Work started on this government project early in 1951, the objective being to develop an engine to power a radio-controlled pilotless aircraft which was being designed and developed for the Ministry of Supply by M.L. Aviation of White Waltham, Berkshire. This small aircraft, to be known as the U120D, would be a high wing monoplane of stressed skin aluminium alloy construction with a wingspan of 12 ft, an overall length of $12\frac{1}{2}$ ft and a weight of 472 lb. Its airspeed in level flight was expected to be in excess of 200 mph with a flight duration of 45 minutes. Its purpose would be to provide an aerial target for ground-to-air gunnery practice and also it would be used for air-to-air firing and radar plotting practice.

The Vincent engine which became the celebrated Picador began life as a normal 'store-requisitioned' 'Black Shadow'; the main feature of the development of the engine being fuel injection, required to eliminate any possibility of fuel starvation when the aircraft was in flight and, above all, when it was blasted into the air by rockets. Another feature of the development was a right-angled bevel drive reduction gear for the 4 ft 6 in fixed pitch wooden airscrew. This was to be driven at half crankshaft speed, a centrifugal-type governor inter-connected with the throttles to prevent the engine from over-revving when the aircraft was in a dive, and an altitude mixture control to keep the fuel-to-air ratio correct.

The engine, as noted, was based on a Black Shadow (a race development of the Series B Rapide—see later chapters), but at the first series of tests, big-end seizures were a problem. After a number of modifications, which included Vincent Lightning camshafts and TT magneto, the engine was still producing too low power for the

Ministry, so it was completely rebuilt to full Lightning specification using 32 mm carbs, 7/11 pistons, making the compression 12.72 (front cylinder) and 12.73 (rear cylinder), the full power curves being achieved with different lengths of exhaust pipe. There was then so much power going through the main shafts that the drive side used to move in the fly wheel, so they were welded in. The Lightning, incidentally, was the racing version of the Rapide.

By the autumn of 1952, after a period of sustained activity, ML Aviation said they would be ready for flight trials by the end of the year, to take place in the Libyan desert in the interests of safety. Jack Lazenby represented the Vincent factory and flew out in January 1953. It was all very secretive, the desert site being kept under guard 24 hours a day by uniformed Arabs. The first flight was a disaster, the aircraft crashing and being damaged beyond repair. When launched it climbed at such a steep angle that, when the rockets burnt out at about 150 ft, it stalled and dived almost vertically into the ground. There were a number of failures, both on this first and subsequent flight trials, before things started to go well, but the project was scrapped by the government in 1957.

The Vincent factory at Stevenage built 42 Picador engines and following normal aircraft practice all external parts were anodised, and the completed engines were coated with anarco varnish. The last batch had fully waterproofed Scintella magnetos, this being achieved by a rubber moulding around the magneto body and the HT leads. The main bearings had positive locking, being held in position by plates screwed to the outside of the bearing housing and locating on two flats ground on the bearing outer race. Double start oil pump worm drives were also fitted. During the flying, engines were lost in the sea and a number were written off owing to crashes. The remaining engines and spares were later sold by public auction, the majority being acquired by the London dealers Deeprose Brothers Ltd, who offered them to the public at the incredibly low price of £70 each.

The Picador project is significant to the Vincent story. Had it been successful and had the Air Ministry ordered engines in quantity, there is little doubt that the production of Vincent motor cycles would have continued for many more years. As it was, though the engine was efficient and reliable enough, the project never overcame its radio control problems and died prematurely.

The Picador engine was a tuned-up version of the Black Shadow unit which was specifically modified for aircraft installation. The 50 degrees V-twin air-cooled geared Poppet valve normally aspirated engine had two cylinders, 80 mm × 90 mm bore and stroke, 998 swept volume and a compression ratio of 11.5:1. The engine had a dry weight of 197 lb with a performance at sea level of 65 bhp at 5,000 rpm.

Ironically, for a company famous for its motor cycles years after its demise, it was to be an industrial engine which the factory turned to for salvation some six years after work was first started on the Picador unit. But, as described in the final chapter, it was not enough to save the proud factory.

Left *George Brown (number 87) at Cadwell Park with the 'speedway special' Vincent with girder forks in 1946* (Cliff Brown).

Above *The Vincent hybrid—non-standard factory parts include brakes and seat and absence of normal tank lettering. Note also the war-time light unit* (Motor Cycle Weekly).

Below *The first production Series B Rapide on its way to the Argentine by air in 1946* (Ted Davis).

24

Above *Arthur Bourne takes the Vincent 1000 on test in 1946, with Philip Vincent looking on* (Cliff Brown).

Below *Vincent-HRD Rapide B, 1946* (Motor Cycle Weekly).

Right *A famous picture from the vintage days of Vincent. Phil Irving (centre) and Cliff Brown (extreme left) with well-known pre-war racer Denis Minett (extreme right) and the Vincent's Australian agent and son, with the Standard Rapide of 1947* (Cliff Brown).

Below right *Cliff Brown with the first production sidecar outfit, 1947* (Cliff Brown).

Below far right *George Brown, who later became the father of British sprinting, racing to another victory on the Cadwell Special at Shelsey Walsh. It was powered by the 500 cc 'speedway' engine* (Motor Cycle Weekly).

Above *Vincent's engine assembly section in the Number 1 factory, circa 1948* (Bruce).
Below *The frame assembly section of the Vincent factory at Stevenage as it was in the late 1940s* (Motor Cycle Weekly).

Above *A vital part of the Vincent set-up as it was in the 1940s—the test-bed in the test house* (Cliff Brown).

Below *The Number 2 factory at Fishers Green, Stevenage, occupied by the Vincent company from 1946, but demolished in 1980* (Cliff Brown).

Left *The twin-cylinder Rapide of 1948, fitted with touring mudguards* (Cliff Brown).

Below left *The perfectly standard test house Comet of 1948* (Cliff Brown).

Bottom left *An historic picture as Rollie Free makes his unique record attempt at the Bonneville Salt Flats on the Black Lightning in 1948.*

Above right *Ted Davis pulls in to refuel his Series B Rapide during the Leinster 200 race in May 1948* (Independent Newspapers).

Right *An unusual view of the 1948 Black Lightning showing the unusually slim profile* (Ted Davis).

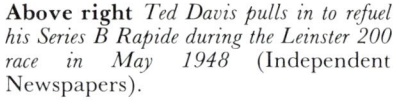

Far right *The Black Shadow, from an unusual angle* (Motor Cycle Weekly).

Above *Record breaking in Belgium, 1948, showing Phil Irving (left) and Rene Millhoux (seated) with the famous Gunga Din. Irving crashed and broke his wrist riding over and the machine had to be rebuilt in Belgium* (Motor Cycle Weekly).

Below *The engine section of the 1949 Vincent Black Shadow* (Motor Cycle Weekly).

Machines for the connoisseur

Vincent-HRD emerged from six years of war in better shape, perhaps, than might have been feared. Ministry contracts had produced useful profit and, as the business began to move back into motor cycle production, the firm was employing more than 400 people (compared with little more than a dozen when war came) and had almost doubled its workshop capacity. More substantial factories, pre-war, had fared less well and some were to disappear for ever.

Even so, moving back to motor cycle production after the war was not easy. Raw materials were in short supply, it was almost impossible to get components when they were required and at the right price and quality, credit facilities were limited and the company was short of capital.

However, as the war had swung decisively in the Allies' favour, Philip Vincent had looked constructively to the future, getting together with Phil Irving to work on a post-war successor to the Series A Rapide. Ambition ran high, though the aim was simple and uncluttered: to produce a better touring motor cycle than anyone else. It would have to be capable, with tuning, of an exceptional top speed and here they had a head start, for the pre-war Series A had been generally recognised at the time as the fastest production motor cycle on the road. Impressive cruise capability was also mandatory, along with de luxe specification throughout. If not altogether conventional in looks, it would need to be handsome to match the pure strain of its pedigree, and the response to its immaculate performance over the entire range should be capably relaxed and easy, the hallmark of all thoroughbreds. The new machine would also have to overcome the problem of the proprietary clutch and gearbox which had undermined the reputation of the Series A, often slipping badly and burning out.

It all took a long time and there were problems and disappointments on the way. But what eventually emerged was a motor cycle of rare distinction. Alongside the Series A, the Series B was

1948: the first production Black Shadow. (Ted Davis).

The famous name forever to be associated with Vincent—Phil Irving (Cliff Brown).

far more refined, practical, cleaner and impressive in just about every department. If, at an easy 110 mph at 45 bhp it was no quicker than its predecessor, it was certainly no slower. Tested on September 19 1946, the first Series B production Rapide was sent out to Vincent's agents in Buenos Aires and was a sensation. Orders soon began to arrive at the factory in such relatively high numbers that, according to Philip Vincent, they were never fully met before manufacture stopped.

There is no doubt that the big-twin high-camshaft 1946 Vincent-HRD Series B Rapide was an exciting and exceptional motor cycle. It differed fundamentally from the earlier model by using the engine as a stressed part of the frame, this being achieved by bolting special lugs to the frame with long studs passing through the cylinder to the crankcase. Vincent and Irving were concerned to save weight for performance considerations and also to compensate for a stronger and heavier gearbox which they needed to fit. That is why they used aluminium for the cylinder heads, for the sleeves which went round iron liners for the cylinders, and (with bronze) for the valve guides. The weight-saving brief was meticulously observed and was so successful that the Series B was by far the world's fastest standard production motor cycle. Its manageable power gave it a realistic, not merely a theoretical, top speed of 112 mph (180 km/h) on the road, and its acceleration was breathtaking. Roadholding and steering were impeccable, braking

was good (one reliable test halted it in just $22\frac{1}{2}$ ft from 30 mph), it was quiet and flexible and the overall superior finish of the machine helped to make it a seriously tempting proposition for the enthusiast, despite a British price tag of £290 in 1946. Even that price left Vincent insufficient margin to include some of his original ideas, including stainless steel wheel rims and petrol tank, a felt-lined tooltray mounted inside a maroon dual seat, and a novel footrest which moved out of the way when the kickstarter was used. It was a handsome machine and distinguished by a petrol tank prestigiously painted black with a gold leaf outline. This unconventional design proved capable of handling up to around 120 bhp from highly tuned versions of the basic engine. It was this clutch arrangement which permitted the concept of the assembly being a stressed structured member in place of a conventional frame, and thereby allowing Vincent to dispense with three frame tubes in his desire to jettison as much surplus weight as possible. The elimination of the front down tubes meant that the angle between the cylinders could be opened up to 50 degrees and this in turn enabled production magnetos to be fitted and a shortening of the wheelbase from the $58\frac{1}{2}$ in of the Series A to the neater 56 in.

The Series B frame was ideal for the simple and effective de-coking and overhauling of the engine. You just hoisted the bike on to the rear stand, inserted a box under the engine, and if you wanted to de-coke the cylinder heads, took out two cylinder head bolts and a rear spring box bolt. If you also took out the rear swinging arm bolt you could lift the whole engine away from the frame for an engine overhaul in about a quarter of an hour, with none of the heavy machine pulling and pushing necessary with a normal tubular type frame. Advanced details included the dynamo drive, the dual seat and bilateral prop stands which could be combined as a front stand to support the engine.

The first prototype Series B Rapide was shown to the Press in early 1946, with an unenamelled tank and a few minor specified parts still missing. But with the fitting of the Series A dampers at the rear end and other final touches, it was soon completed and ready for running on Saturday April 27 1946. Graham Walker and Arthur Bourne, the then editors of *Motor Cycle* and *Motor Cycling* respectively, were given the privilege of early rides. Bourne was impressed with its 'magnificent road holding' and he thought it acted as nimbly as a 500 in traffic, and Walker thought it was extremely compact and that it handled very well. The atmosphere is remembered by Cliff Brown, an important Vincent 'boffin' for many years.

'I moved over to Number 2 factory which Mr Vincent had been allotted by the Ministry in late 1945. I made some space in a corner of the factory with benches and welding screens left by the previous occupant for the assembly of engines. Ted Hampshire had the centre of the factory for the assembly of the frames on a railway, helped by Jack Lazenby. There was no heating so we used 10-gallon oil drums for coke fires to keep warm.'

The first six engines were built and the complete machines finished in September 1946. Brown said he used to push them up the inside of the factory to start them because they were still a little tight. Then Philip Vincent would ride them round to free them off before tester Jim Sugg took them out on the road. Brown said that the first one or two in the initial batch suffered big-end seizures and he stripped them down for inspection and found that the crank pins had not sufficient clearance for the side plates. 'So Mr Irving had the drawing rectified and after that we had no further trouble,' he explained.

After being shown successfully at an exhibition in the Argentine this first Rapide was handed over to the local motor cycle racer and on its first outing finished ahead of the field.

In the next few years the Vincent name was to gain an international reputation, not only as an immaculate touring machine, but as a sporting and racing bike. The transition from the normal Series B Rapide to its super-sporting version, the incredible Black Shadow, was master-minded initially by Phil Irving, George Brown and his brother, Cliff, and later with the addition of Philip Vincent himself, though it is doubtful if the outstanding success of the Black Shadow could have been predicted when the first quiet moves were made.

It really all began when Philip Vincent crashed a Rapide he was testing, the engine seizing when he was travelling at 110 mph. While he was away recovering from his crash the Brown brothers and Irving took one of the first Rapides which had been discarded by the test department, 'breathed' on it, and, as the 'Gunga Din', George rode it to numerous successes in road races and hill climbs. Inspired by this success, Philip Vincent then became enthusiastic about developing a sports version of the Rapide. With it he could visualise the realisation of a career-long dream, extending back some 20 years, of developing a touring bike with a top speed of 120 mph and an easy cruise speed of 100 mph. More significant perhaps was the sales potential he saw in such a model, but joint managing director Frank Walker did not share his enthusiasm. Vincent was determined and, aided by Phil Irving, George and

Cliff Brown, the project took shape under wraps in the Vincent factory and was too far advanced to abandon everything when Walker finally got wind of what was going on.

Named the Black Shadow, two machines were made initially and the model was openly announced in February 1948. It was to become an incomparable machine and for years remained the world's fastest standard production motor cycle, long after production ceased. Its performance was phenomenal—up to 90 mph in less than 15 seconds and a top speed of 128 mph. *Motor Cycling* said road conditions and the rider's abilities were the only restrictions! In the end more Black Shadows were sold than Rapides, from which it was derived, and it acquired a phenomenal reputation for its speed, acceleration, all round quality, reliability, fuel consumption and overall performance. It was the aristocrat of motor cycles and a masterpiece of engineering. It quickly became a legend and more than 30 years afterwards it still retains an enviable place in motor cycle history as one of the industry's truly classic machines.

In 1948 the Black Shadow cost £381, but for that the buyer secured a machine unrivalled for its performance by any other two-wheeler and it was faster than the majority of cars then available at considerably more money.

Special features of the Black Shadow were high compression pistons with ratios of 7.3:1, bigger carburettors attached to bronze flanges, highly polished combustion chambers, valve rockers and connecting rods, an exceptionally accurate and legible speedometer, specially designed cast-iron and ribbed brake drums, and a whole catalogue of 'fine detail' items including a full range of adjustments for the gear lever, brake pedal, foot-rests and handlebars. The name came from the appearance of the machine, which looked sleek, potent and stealthily exciting with the exterior of the engine, cylinder barrels and heads, crankcase, brakes, etc, finished in all-black. The quality of finish was superb and serviceable. Both Irving and Vincent rejected telescopic forks and the first models were fitted with Brampton front forks, these being replaced by Vincent's own Girdraulics on the Series C models which were introduced in 1948/9. A quick simultaneous adjustment of the trail and spring rate was possible for solo or sidecar work.

The potential of the standard Black Shadow was exploited in 1948 with the introduction of a top-of-the-range tuned version called the Black Lightning. At £400 including tax it was £85 dearer than the standard Black Shadow and incorporated a number of special features, including, in addition to the specially tuned engine, racing high-lift camshafts, a choice of high compression pistons, 2 in exhaust

Gunga Din with the rider who made it famous, George Brown (extreme right), and the remainder of the development team—Cliff Brown, Phil Irving and Mike Eggington.

pipes, alloy wheel rims, an 8,000 rpm rev counter and a close-ratio gearbox for quicker gear changing. Although the Black Lightning was available for almost seven years, from 1948 right through to the end of Vincent motor cycle production in 1955, only about 20 were made, but it was one of these superlative machines which took New Zealander Russell Wright to a new outright motor cycle world record in 1955 at 185 mph (289 km/h). Streamlined, but unsupercharged, this Vincent Black Lightning was to be one of the last traditional types of motor cycle to secure the outright record. A year later, after losing the honour to Wilhelm Herz on an NSU, Wright tried unsuccessfully to regain the record, just failing to reach 200 mph on the unblown Black Lightning.

These post-war Vincent twins—the Black Shadow and Black Lightning—were inspiring, high-performance classics which were to earn a special place in motor cycle history. New features of the first Series C Rapides, introduced at about the same time as the Black Lightning with its alcohol-fuelled engine, were improved rear suspension, incorporating a new damper fitted between the two rear spring boxes, and Vincent's own Girdraulic forks. The Stevenage factory had not rushed into new fork design immediately after the war, as many factories had done, Irving and Vincent taking their time in formulating their ideas. In the end, both dismissed telescopics which they considered distinctly unsuitable for the Vincent design. Instead they built on the best features of the girder principle using light alloy blades, one-piece (instead of loose) links, and featuring hydraulic damping. Twin, long coil springs, in compression only and contained in separate boxes, were used.

Meantime, the popular Comets and Meteors had continued almost unchanged, though the Rapide had made the Comet Special virtually unnecessary by 1938. That year's Series B production models had included a much improved TT Replica.

Whereas before the war Vincents had put two 500 cc Comet engines together to form the 1,000 cc Series A Rapide, after the war they worked the system in reverse, halving the big-twin (which by this time had been successfully cleaned up by 'losing' the external oil feed pipes) and bringing out a new-style 500 cc Comet. It was, of course, a single-cylinder 500 cc ohv machine, with valve operation by high camshafts and short push-rods. It had a magneto ignition, chain transmission and four-speed Burman gearbox. The backbone member of the frame incorporated the oil tank, and the rear swinging-fork suspension pivoted from rear of the gearbox plates. Hydraulically damped girder forks were used.

The Series C Comet (and the Series B Meteor) were launched at the 1948 London Show—the Comet being tuned almost to Black Shadow specification, the Meteor almost to Rapide specification. The Series B Meteor continued in production until 1950, the Series C Comet until 1954.

Shortly after production of these 1948 Comets began, Philip Vincent asked George and Cliff Brown to produce a tuned version suitable for racing and the Grey Flash was the result. Its first race outing was in May 1949, when George Brown finished third in a 15-lap race at Eppynt. Later Brown took one of the five 'works' Grey Flashes, produced during the short time it was in production, to Gransden and reached an impressive 119 mph on 'pool' petrol. It was this performance which boosted the morale of the Vincent works team entered that year in the Senior TT, though the Grey Flash was withdrawn at the end of August 1950, the reason given being the need to concentrate on production models and the extravagant use of factory time and skill which the Grey Flash demanded. About 30 Grey Flashes were made and John Surtees was one rider who raced them successfully.

In 1949 another landmark in Vincent history occurred. The HRD initials were deleted from the factory's models, a new Vincent scroll taking their place. This happened after a visit to America by Philip Vincent during which he discovered a certain amount of confusion among potential buyers who wondered if the initials HRD had anything to do with Harley-Davidson. In 1952 the name of the company was changed to Vincent Engineering Company Ltd and then again, because it was discovered that a Scottish company had a similar name, to Vincent Engineers (Stevenage) Ltd.

It was in 1949, too, that Philip Vincent, during a visit to the United States, looked into the commercial possibilities of fitting a Rapide engine into an Indian Super Chief frame. The idea came originally from the Indian company itself when Vincent accepted an invitation to visit the company on his annual trip to the United States.

· The Indian 1,200 cc was clumsy and overweight for its sidevalve engine and reached only 80 mph at maximum. With modifications the Rapide engine could be used perhaps to open up a completely new market. Vincent arranged for two Indian Super Chief machines to be shipped to Stevenage and the Rapide unit was fitted successfully into one of them. The machine was tagged the Vindian and the prospects for the future success of the unlikely liaison were sufficient for the factory to be talking about weekly production figures of, perhaps, 50 machines. Phil Irving, along with George and Clifford Brown, with Bill Munsden doing the welding, made an exceptionally neat job of altering the big Indian frame to accommodate the powerful Rapide engine and George tested it on the Gransden road at a speed in excess of 100 mph. It appeared to have possibilities, but like too many ideas with which the Vincent factory was to be associated, it did not amount to anything commercially. Philip Vincent reckoned that the Indian factory became too enthusiastic about selling the standard Rapides and Black Shadows on the American market to bother about complicated hybrids like the Vindian.

Apparently the prototype Vindian was shipped out to the Indian factory at Springfield and, as other events took priority at Stevenage, was never seen again in Britain, or heard much of in the United

States. Phil Irving left the Vincent Company at the end of 1949 and, according to one source, took the other machine with him, after changing it back to its original specification and fitting a sidecar to it, back to Australia where he was reported to have sold it two years later. There appears to be some doubt, however, because Clifford Brown insists on the authenticity of another version of the Vindian saga, maintaining that one of the Indian machines to arrive from America was never even taken out of its crate. He says he fitted the original Indian engine into the other machine before it was shipped back to the United States, along with the second machine. He insists that only one Indian bike was altered to fit the Vincent engine and the bikes had to be sent back to the USA within a limited time as import tax had not been paid on them.

For a factory which was so totally identified with performance motor cycles, Vincent's decision in 1952 and '53 to concern itself with 48 cc cycle attachment units was nothing short of heresy. As the first signs of a slackening in the post-war boom in the sales of motor cycles were beginning to show, Philip Vincent felt diversification would help his company to survive. Motorising your pedal cycle with a small pop-pop unit was beginning to catch on in Britain, after the idea had been popularised years before on the Continent, and there was a huge anticipated demand for them at a time when Philip Vincent visited the electrical firm of H. Miller and Company. They were about to put a major effort into their new Firefly cyclomotor and Vincent was not slow to see a possible opportunity when he was asked if he would be interested in making and marketing the cyclomotor, since they felt the project might become too big to handle themselves.

In 1953 the Vincent company offered just the unit for £25 and then the whole machine in 1955 for less than £40. Philip Vincent considered it to be a very worthy machine of its type and well engineered, but it never hit the market at the hoped-for level and, although some 3,000 Firefly units were sold, the project collapsed once sales began to fall away. What really killed it off was a serious problem which Vincent maintained he inherited from Millers. Rubber bonding of the drive roller on to the shaft sleeve was not effective and the complaints grew in almost direct proportion to sales increases. Vincent was rightly sensitive to his firm's reputation for quality, but he gave the suppliers too long to correct the fault and when they did not come through with the solution, only then called in the expertise at the Avon company. It was by this time too late and much damage had been done. But by 1954 and '55 the sad Firefly experience had been virtually forgotten as Vincents took over the distribution in

Britain of the mopeds and lightweight motor cycles being manufactured by NSU in Germany. These NSU Quicklys were sound machines, with fine lines and good performance and they found a ready market in the UK. The machine weighed 80 lb and had a two-stroke engine, two speed gearbox and was clean, neat and smooth.

It should be said that the contract for selling and servicing of the popular Quickly moped in Britain, from the German NSU factory, was only ever scheduled for one year, but that year was perhaps one of the most successful and certainly one of the most active in Vincent's short history. They were soon selling about 1,000 a month (at almost £60 each) and within a period of six months had delivered around 20,000 machines. The agency for the Quickly was linked to a deal by which Vincent undertook the manufacture and marketing in Britain of several other NSU models. These bikes were basic NSUs, but with a number of special features intended to make them more appealing to the British bike-buying public. NSU models undertaken by Vincents were the 98 cc overhead valve Fox, the 125 cc two-stroke Fox, the 250 cc Max with an overhead camshaft over-square engine which developed 18 bhp at 6,650 rpm and which had a top speed of around 80 mph, pressed steel backbone frame and unit construction, and a 200 cc flat-piston two-stroke called the Lux. The 250 was a particularly interesting and well finished bike, with excellent specifications and was good to look at, but although a prototype was displayed at the Earls Court show in 1953 and featured in the factory catalogue, it never went into production at Stevenage because the cost of the German parts made it prohibitively expensive in the UK.

This part of the arrangement never worked out totally satisfactorily and sales were disappointing, though the production of the Foxes continued until the autumn of 1955, more than 18 months after the Quickly moped arrangement ended. Philip Vincent at one time admitted that the factory, including himself, were so blinkered by the success of the Quickly moped that they might not have given as much effort and concentration as they should have done to the marketing of the other models. They literally could sell as many of the little machines as they could get from Germany—and still the waiting lists grew. It was such an outstanding success that at the end of the year NSU had seen enough to make them decide to take over things themselves and form their own company to handle the business.

It was in the early 1950s that Philip Vincent began to work out plans for the production of a three-wheel car. The overall sales of motor cycles in Britain were not encouraging as the high post-war demand had been satisfied, and Philip Vincent was anxious to find another outlet for his Rapide engines so that he could keep up production at economic levels. The vehicle was first successfully road tested in 1955 and after a few months' delay was handed over to Ted Davis for development. Although with the standard Rapide engine the three-wheeler could go at almost 90 mph, Davis was concerned to improve this performance and replaced the standard engine with the highly tuned Lightning which had been installed in George Brown's earlier successful Gunga Din.

Eventually he got it up to about 115 mph and used it later in a number of sprints, where it performed well. The three-wheeler was offered to the public towards the end of 1955 and, although it captured a good deal of interest, the price of £500 scared off potential buyers. Although the project failed to solve Philip Vincent's problem of utilising his production and assembly resources more effectively, he was enthusiastic about the vehicle he had produced. It had three-wheel independent suspension with hydraulic damping and in the prototype incorporated a large number of motor cycle parts including engine, clutch, power transmission and gearbox. This was an attractive proposition from a commercial point of view and the project generally seemed to have a lot going for it. The company, for once, had enough time to work out carefully all the detail and to give the vehicle a comprehensive testing, but on this occasion Vincent's initiative was to be sabotaged by the company's own parlous economic condition. To make room for the car body-building programme it would have been necessary to extend the works significantly. Moreover, the development needed investment at a level which the relatively small Vincent company simply could not muster. In mind was a super sports version incorporating a Black Lightning engine which would have boosted the top speed to about 120 mph and incorporated a number of exciting and interesting features. Alas, what appeared to be yet another promising project mounted by the Vincent factory was allowed to wither and the three-wheeler never got into production.

It was largely because of his pre-occupation with the Picador project that Philip Vincent was not able to think seriously about a successor to the Series C models until 1954. In the intervening years, rivals had pushed ahead with improvements, but the talented Stevenage unit were able to produce their Series D machines and what emerged was a startling development.

But before that, a remarkable endurance feat on a Vincent machine captures our attention.

Above *George Brown at Ramsey Hairpin on the 1,000 cc Vincent in the 1948 Clubman's TT on the Isle of Man. He finished sixth behind Ted Davis* (Motor Cycle Weekly).

Right *Ted Davis working on a 1949 Series B Black Shadow* (Ted Davis).

Above left *A Series C Black Shadow of 1949* (Ted Davis).

Above *Size comparisons: the power and complexity of the Series B Black Shadow of 1949 and the Firefly cycle attachment engine of 1953* (Ted Davis).

Left *A Vincent Black Shadow 1949 vintage with a Steib sidecar* (Ted Davis).

Above right *George Brown outside the Vincent Test House in the famous Gunga Din in the late 1940s.*

Right *Vincent twins at the Number 1 factory ready for despatch in 1949* (Cliff Brown).

99

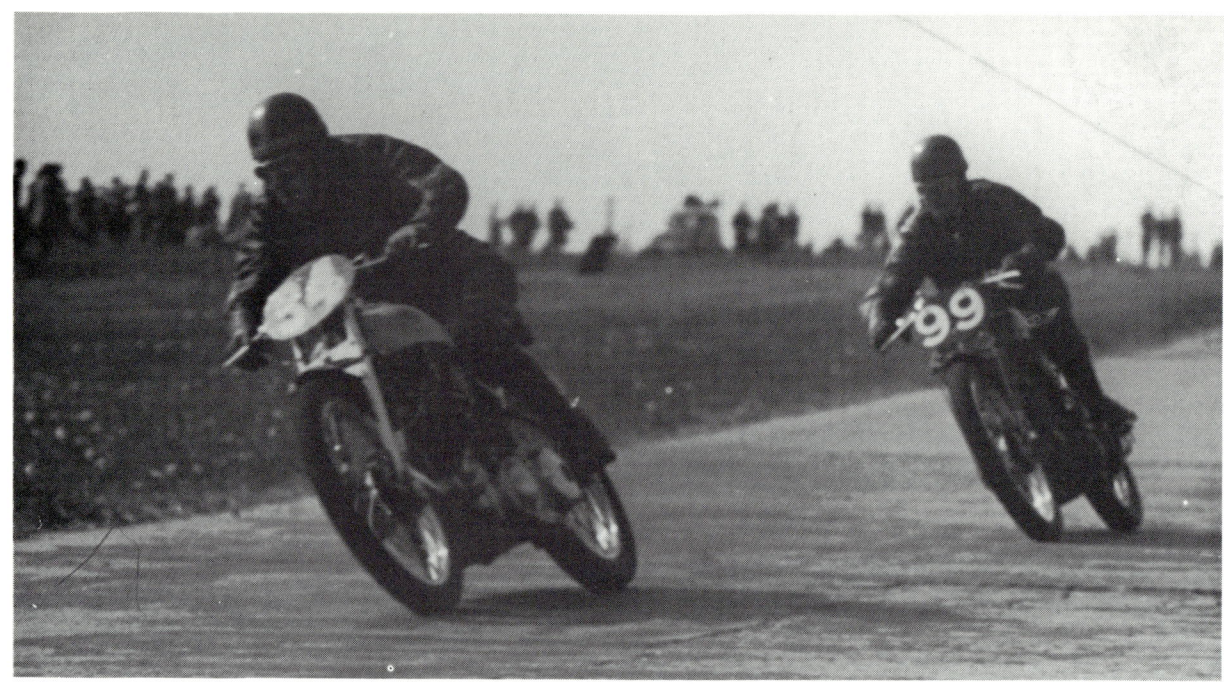

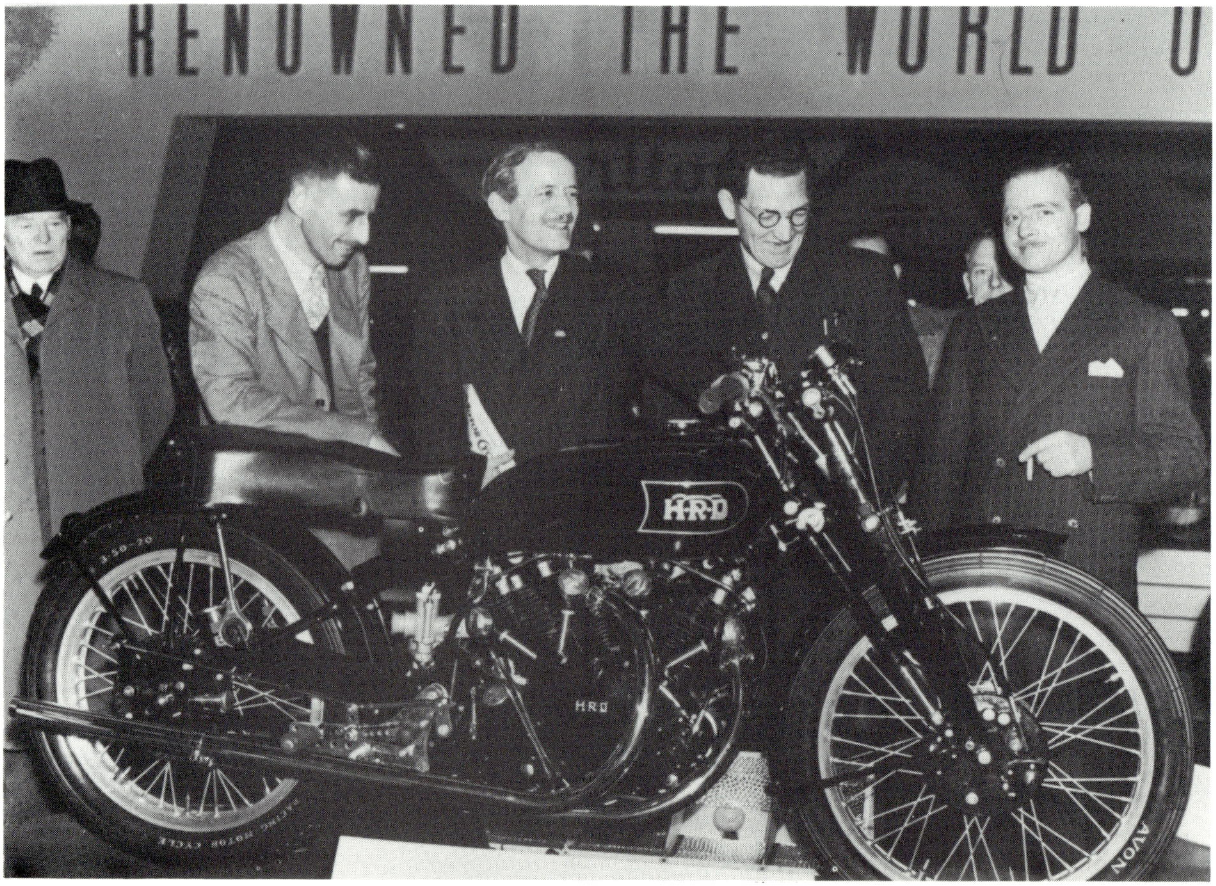
RENOWNED THE WORLD
H·R·D
HRD
RACING MOTOR CYCLE
AVON

Left *Ted Davis leads George Brown, both on Black Lightnings, at Haddenham in 1949* (Ted Davis).

Below left *The famous Black Lightning at Earls Court in 1949 with sales manager Ken Mainwaring, Philip Vincent, Phil Irving and George Brown* (Ted Davis).

Top right *The Series C Black Shadow of 1949* (Motor Cycle Weekly).

Above right *The Series C Black Lightning of 1949* (Motor Cycle Weekly).

Right *The 500 cc Comet of 1949* (Motor Cycle Weekly).

Above left *George Brown racing the new Grey Flash at Scarborough for the first time, in 1949* (G.C. Schofield).

Left *Haddenham in 1949 with Ted Davis riding the Black Lightning* (Ted Davis).

Above *On the works trials version of the Comet in 1950, with George Brown the master* (Home Counties Newspapers).

Right *The 1950 Grey Flash at Ted Davis' Letchworth home* (Ted Davis).

Close-up of an ex-works Grey Flash (Ted Davis).

Vincent Black Shadow of 1950.

The 998 cc Vincent Black Lightning of 1950.

The 100,000-mile Enduro

If anyone put Vincent claims to the test it was Tony Rose. Nationally known weight-lifter, body-builder (and still active as such) and high-diver, Tony was a private detective in 1951, a motor cycle enthusiast with membership of the Vincent-HRD Club, and the proud possessor of a new Vincent Black Shadow. He was also something of an adventurer and once Philip Vincent had assured him that a Shadow ought to be capable of doing 100,000 miles without major replacements becoming necessary (admittedly Tony had specifically asked the question at the Earls Court Motor Cycle Show that year), he decided to set out to prove it.

At first in solo form and later with a sidecar for more stability, Tony rode the Black Shadow—which was a perfectly standard machine—a distance equivalent to four times round the world (an incredible 100,000 miles) in what was probably the

world's most extraordinary road test. It took over a year, since the marathon had to be fitted around Tony's assignments as a private investigator, but it proved convincingly the remarkable reliability of the Vincent machine, which came through the test with flying colours.

The Vincent Owners' Club sponsored the expedition and with fitness-fanatic Tony Rose in the saddle, the Vincent MKB 465 set off from the Stevenage works with 11,380 miles already on the clock. During December 1951 a further 7,380 miles were added without trouble of any kind. Two months later Tony rode into Leeds concerned that a

The phenomenal Vincent 100,000-mile marathon with endurance rider Tony Rose (extreme left), sidecar passenger Jim Reegan (extreme right), and A.C.F. Warner of Filtrate Ltd (Yorkshire Post).

valve guide might be 'picking up'. Squirting Colloidal Petroyle into the carburettor air intakes with the motor at a fast tick-over did the trick and no further problems of this kind were encountered. At this stage Tony had already completed more than 22,000 miles, cruising at between 80 and 100 miles an hour. In the meantime a Blacknell Bullet sidecar had been attached after Tony had separated from the Vincent when striking a patch of ice and skuffing down the road on the seat of his pants.

By March 1952 he had travelled almost 28,000 miles and although no attempt was made to find top speeds, Tony said he had recorded over 110 mph solo and an equally impressive 93 mph with the sidecar attached. At this stage the machine was behaving perfectly and oil consumption was normal.

At 33,000 miles, in April, slight piston slap was reported, though oil consumption was working out at about one pint every 350 miles. Later that month an oil pipe came adrift almost wrecking the test. Tony must have ridden for at least eight miles before discovering the problem and getting the pipe replaced. The engine was still performing well after 38,000 miles, though using a little oil (one pint each 200 miles), but with improved weather Tony put 8,000 miles on the clock in May and a further 8,500 in June to bring him within sight of the 50,000 miles half-way mark by early July.

He had been making his way towards Stevenage to have the machine serviced at the Vincent works. Astonishingly, the mechanics, who, incidentally, included John Surtees, found the oil pipe adrift and no oil in the tank. They reckoned he must have ridden the machine like that for about ten miles. Two broken piston rings in the rear cylinder and a broken valve spring were replaced, together with clutch linkings, tyres and chains. Then the marathon was continued in all weathers and under some of the most appalling conditions. At one point the sidecar wheel collapsed and a number of spokes were smashed. Later a Swallow Commando sidecar replaced the Blacknell Bullet. Still later a two-seater sidecar was fitted and Vincent enthusiast Jim Regan joined the marathon, riding passenger and also driving. Occasionally Tony's wife and young children accompanied him for short spells.

This really was putting the Vincent to a most severe test because, when Philip Vincent had responded affirmatively to Tony Rose's challenge, he had only anticipated the Black Shadow being ridden solo for the 100,000 miles. No matter, eight thousand miles were added in August. In September, when Tony detached the sidecar for a spell of solo riding, he could still cruise comfortably at 80 mph, though at 112 mph he reported that the engine was a 'trifle noisier'. At this point the Vincent had been ridden for an average of 220 miles a day for ten months.

At 75,000 miles oil consumption was still only one pint for every 200 miles, but it was at this point that Tony began to suspect big-end trouble, as the engine became noisier. With 5,000 more miles showing on the dial, Tony's suspicions mounted and for the first time he began to have serious doubts about reaching the 100,000 miles target. But he decided at this stage, with only 15,000 to go, that his only option was to carry on. At 88,000 miles, in December, the roads were hazardous and the sidecar was refitted to give more stability on the slippery roads, though cruising speed continued at around 70 mph.

Tony was scheduled to finish the 100,000-mile marathon at Banff in Scotland, near the home of the Vincent Club magazine editor Rab Cook, but with co-driver Jim Regan he literally had to claw his way north from his hometown of Liverpool. Driving snow and a raging 120 mph tempest uprooted trees and sent the riders round lengthy and tortuous detours, sometimes forcing them to drive across rough country. At other times they had to hack their way through fallen trees to clear a path. One enormous gust of wind almost flung them into Loch Lomond. Road conditions were appalling with sheet ice and snow creating frightening hazards. A noisy engine, had they been able to hear it through the buffeting weather conditions, was now the least of Tony's worries. After battling the whole of Saturday January 31 1953, the pair reached Banff that evening, to complete the marathon ride.

However, that was not quite the end of the story, for on the way north the speedometer cable broke and the machine's instruments showed a shortfall on the 100,000. It was only a technicality, but to put the test beyond any doubt, Tony, after a brief sleep, returned south and journeyed through the night to reach the Filtrate Oil factory at Leeds. The following day Tony and Jim resumed their journey south to Stevenage to complete their mission and have the machine checked over by the Vincent factory mechanics. The historic 100,000-mile reading had shown on the clock while the intrepid travellers had been in the Carlisle area.

The 'big-end' problem was found to be nothing worse than fatigued engine shock-absorber springs which allowed the shock-absorber cams to rise rather rapidly. Of the total 100,000 miles, 80,000 were completed with the sidecar attached. Oil was changed regularly and Tony's sensible attitude in not over-revving the engine and allowing it to warm up for 12 miles before going on to full throttle obviously did much to preserve the engine's condition.

The entire expedition had been completed at a daily average in excess of 200 miles. Engine wear, as monitored at the end of the expedition by Vincent factory specialists, was as follows:

Layshaft 1st gear	Bore wear 0.0006 in
Layshaft 2nd gear	Bore wear 0.00025 in
Layshaft journal wear	0.0005 in
Cylinder barrels, bore wear:	Front 0.0035 in to 0.004 in
	Rear 0.0025 in to 0.0035 in
Crankpin roller tracks wear:	0.0003 in
Con rod big end liner wear:	0.0004 in
Rocker pin wear:	0.003 in average
Rocker bearing wear:	0.003 in average

Carbon: The imprint 'Specialloid' was clearly legible on piston crowns.

About three months after the completion of the test the Series C Black Shadow which Tony Rose had bought new for £415 was sold to a local dealer in Lancashire for just £175. Early in 1981 when writing this book I asked Tony Rose, who later worked for Granada Television as an announcer and later still as a motor auctioneer, what became of the famous bike. 'The Vincent-HRD works rebuilt it before it was sold to Lifes Motors in Southport,' he said.

Tony also said that the victory celebration at Stevenage was a superb line-up of all the top motor cycling journalists of the day and he had telephone calls at home saying he had put the 1,000 cc bike on the map at last and the day of the big bike would come. He said he spent the next four days at Stevenage trying to catch up on one year's sleep and nil entertainment over the same period. 'It was a wonderful period and we had a wonderful few days, Philip Vincent ending up getting married to the charming lady from the local,' said Tony, who afterwards rested for six months and trained back to fitness on weights and playing tennis. 'How right we all were, for this period heralded the coming of the superbike and perhaps the special supermen who ride them,' he said.

Putting Vincent to the test

Philip Vincent's policy was to sell motor cycles of exceptional quality, reliability and performance, and although he did not design and build race machinery for a grand prix team in the style of Honda in the 1960s, he was always interested in developing his basic models and offering them to the public as 'specials'. Because of this he maintained a keen interest in performance events and high-speed record attempts and these activities, whether performed by his own factory riders or by outsiders riding Vincent machinery, are important and fascinating features of Vincent history.

Comet Special engines were built in the mid-1930s for the factory's first racing attempts on the Isle of Man, in the Clubman's TT, and, as reported, the first 1,000 cc Vincent twin was raced by George Brown at Brooklands at 113 mph in the rain, while at Donington noted TT rider Ginger Wood, who worked for Vincent-HRD for a time, made a death-defying leap over the top of Melbourne Hill which is talked about to this day.

It should be remembered, too, that it was competition in trials, hill climbs and grass-track races on Vincent-HRD machines powered by Rudge Python and Bantam engines by riders like Peter Fry, John Cockshott, Bill Clarke and Jim Sugg, which directed important attention to Philip Vincent's revolutionary rear wheel springing. An ill-fated banking sidecar which Vincent-HRD produced was also race-inspired. It was special in the sense that the sidecar could be braked independently by the passenger, who could also steer and bank the outfit. The amount of bank was eight

Ted Davis and Erne Allen setting the sidecar lap record of 88.29 mph for Vincent at Boreham, 1952 (Charles Dunne).

degrees to the left and ten degrees to the right. Despite incorporating the first ever dual-brake system and a number of other special features, the idea was abandoned after its unsuccessful debut at Brooklands in 1933.

George Brown symbolised Vincent's racing and record breaking deeds, first on the celebrated Gunga Din which he rode while employed by the Stevenage factory, and later through his privately-owned but Vincent-powered Nero and Super Nero, two of the most famous names in motor cycle racing history. Gunga Din emerged while Philip Vincent was recovering from a 110 mph crash in 1946 and was the product of Phil Irving, George himself and brother Cliff. It was a much developed Rapide engine, which had been discarded by the test department. The machine's first year was so promising that in 1948 it was ridden by Belgian ace René Milhoux at Jabbeke and shattered the existing world standing start kilometre sidecar record and the standing start mile world sidecar record, then standing respectively to Eric Fernihough at 80.49 mph on his Brough Superior (1936) and Ernst Henne at 91.95 mph on his BMW (1932). Milhoux's speeds were 83.5 mph and 94 mph and he set a new Belgian national record solo run at 143 mph. A year later the Belgian again impressively established a number of important records.

In hill climbs and ridden by George Brown, Gunga Din was devastating. Brown, at his first visit to Shelsley Walsh, shattered even the car world by breaking the record for the course with a time of 37.13 seconds and on Vincent-powered machinery, though not always with Gunga Din, he was in a class of his own at this famous hill climb venue, collecting the prize money there for 16 years!

Down the Engineers Straight at Blandford, Brown got 140 mph out of Gunga Din running on methanol and at Dunholme, 135 mph. The record of this famous machine in 1949 alone was nothing short of remarkable. At Ansty, Haddenham, Blandford and numerous other venues, Gunga Din recorded victory after victory, winning the first race to be held at Silverstone since the war, a ten-lap scratch event for solos up to 1,000 cc.

The specification of Gunga Din included the 50-degree V-twin Vincent 1,000 cc ohv engine with valve operation by high-lift camshafts and short push rods, magneto ignition and transmission from primary drive to a four-speed gearbox in unit with engine via triple-row chain with slipper tensioner and with final drive by chain. The frame was of the box-girder backbone type incorporating steering head and oil tank, bolted to cylinder heads; rear suspension by triangulated swinging fork with springs anchored to the rear of the box girder, and Vincent's Girdraulic girder forks were fitted.

Though not significantly altered from the production 1,000 cc models, Gunga Din was, in fact, the prototype of the Black Lightning racer.

Another famous Vincent machine immortalised by George Brown was the 'speedway special', a 500 cc model introduced in an effort to keep the factory busy and as a sales stimulus while the Series B Rapide was being completed. It was never a commercial success and only about a dozen of the engines were sold, but Brown was highly successful on the 500 cc machine. The new engine was uncommonly light at only 54 lb including the magneto and carburettor, and was used with success in speedway by Eric Chitty, the captain of West Ham. In a lighter frame this engine was later raced with success by Brown, initially at a Cadwell Park meeting at which he gave Les Graham on the AJS Porcupine considerable concern, and became known also as the Cadwell Special.

Both George and his brother Cliff were key figures in Vincent 'performance' activity at this time and it was they who produced the tuned version of the Series C Comet for racing, known as the Grey Flash. This 500 cc machine was raced by George for the first time at Eppynt in 1949, the Vincent completing the 15 laps to finish in third place after Les Graham on his AJS 7R, and Sid Barnett on his Triumph twin. John Surtees also rode the Grey Flash successfully while he was an apprentice at the factory and, indeed, had his first victory at the famous Brands Hatch circuit, where he was later to become the uncrowned 'king', with the Vincent model. Vincent subsequently marketed the Grey Flash as a stripped racer, as a standard tourer and also as a touring machine with racing equipment, but all told only about 30 were made before the model was withdrawn only about a year later. The Grey Flash retains a prominent place in Vincent history, however, being the model used by the factory in 1950 in the only concerted official team assault on the TT Races in the post-war years. George Brown was one of the riders, C.J. Williams, C.A. Stevens and Manliffe Barrington the others, but insufficient development work resulting in big-end problems and then gearbox failures made it a dismal experience. Ken Bills, taking over from George Brown, did best, finishing the Senior race in twelfth position.

The Isle of Man experience was not entirely strange to the Vincent factory. They had been there first in 1934, competing with a three-man team in the Senior event. Arthur Tyler reached fourth position, Jack Williams was in seventh place, but these two riders, along with John Carr, all retired with mechanical trouble. These were the days, however, when Vincents were using the JAP engine and, as noted earlier, a series of mix-ups and indecision from the JAP factory were largely responsible for the relatively poor showing. When Vincents returned to the Isle of Man the following year it was with their own power unit. The results were better. Jack Williams finished in seventh place at an average 73.94 mph and Noel Christmas was ninth at 73.26 mph. Privately-entered Vincents carrying Barrington, Croft and Courtney finished eleventh, twelfth and thirteenth, Barrington and Courtney's machines being powered by JAP engines.

The factory's next pre-war effort on the Isle of Man was in 1936 when they mounted an ambitious effort, entering Jack Williams, Manliffe Barrington, Jock Forbes and Jock West on supercharged versions of the Comet-powered Vincents. Little comfort could be gained from pre-race tests at Donington Park, with two supercharged models showing little better performance than the atmospheric counterparts. After disappointing practice outings on the Island, the decision was made to abandon the superchargers and run the machines as conventional models. West was the only Vincent rider to finish, and he had to push his machine home after the primary chain had snapped at Governor's Bridge. But the Vincent was the only machine outside Nortons and Velocettes to finish.

Philip Vincent was never prepared to build special racing machines which were substantially out of context with his production models, but in spite of the trends which put his machinery increasingly at a disadvantage alongside the Nortons, AJSs, Velocettes and others, he entered a works team of three on new Series B TT Replicas, but when all three entries failed to finish he called it a day and was not tempted to have another fling until 1950.

But speed records still attracted him, especially when linked to business opportunities, and so in 1948 he shipped out to America a specially-tuned standard Black Shadow for the experienced American racing driver and motor cyclist Roland Free to make a bid for the American national speed record. Such was the performance of Vincent machinery that the standard Black Shadow models were being timed at more than 120 mph, only some 15 mph slower than the then current American national speed record. When John Edgar, a wealthy American with a passion for motor cycles, heard about this he willingly paid the £50 asked by Philip Vincent for converting the Black Shadow into what became known as the Black Lightning, and engaged Roland Free for the record attempt.

The Black Lightning was fashioned on George Brown's famous Gunga Din and incorporated special Mark 2 camshafts which Phil Irving designed specially. George Brown tested the machine at Gransden and reached 143 mph before the restricted length of the runway forced him to throttle back.

The American national record for the mile stood at 136 mph to a Harley-Davidson ridden by Joe Petrali in 1937 at Daytona, but Roland Free's first run on the salt flats at Bonneville less than three weeks after the machine's arrival in the United States was well within the record time, but the attempt had to be discounted as the Vincent oiled a plug when being set up for the re-run. His second attempt, half an hour later, was successful and the new record was set at a convincing 148 mph. As Philip Vincent had virtually guaranteed a 150 mph performance for the Black Lightning, Rollie Free decided to see if he could push the record to nearer that figure. Wearing only a crash hat, bathing trunks and shoes (his racing leathers had been torn in the earlier record runs), Roland Free was an incredible sight as he raced to a new record of 150.313 mph to become the fastest man on earth on an unsupercharged motor cycle.

This success led Roland Free to an attempt on the ultimate world motor cycle record which then stood to the credit of Ernst Henne, who rode a supercharged streamlined BMW at 173.625 mph. He ordered a new Black Lightning from the Stevenage concern and got an aerodynamicist to design a fibreglass streamlined shell for it. The first attempt was almost a disaster. With the streamlining the Vincent was unstable and it swung violently as Free attempted to control it at around 145 mph. The machine skidded across the salt performing all kinds of uncontrollable gyrations and the rider was lucky to escape with nothing more serious than a salt burn after the machine had slid uncontrollably for 1,000 ft.

He abandoned the streamlining and made a bid for a series of records, immediately exceeding the kilometre and mile records at speeds of 156.77 mph and 156.58 mph. In surface conditions which were far from ideal, he raced the Vincent at 154 mph for ten miles and was on his return run when he was almost overcome with fatigue, but he held on and completed the ten-mile record distance at an average of 152.32 mph. Although his speeds for the ten kilometres and ten miles were better than anything done officially before, the records were not ratified because, to qualify under FIM regulations, they should have been made from a standing start.

It was another Vincent, this time ridden by Joe Simpson, which robbed Roland Free of his mile record with a new average of 160.69 mph, but almost immediately Free retaliated, taking his unstreamlined Black Lightning to a new record of 163.54 mph.

The curious thing about Roland Free, who died in 1981, was his riding style on the Vincent. His record attempts were made with him gripping the bars at arms' length, his body stretched out along the top of the machine with his legs suspended aft. Only when he felt in danger of falling off during the ten-mile record attempt did he clamber back to the normal straddle position.

A less successful record-breaking machine was the Vincent made to the special order of Reg Dearden in 1950. It was said to have cost around £5,000, a huge sum then, but Dearden's ambition to take the machine to Utah in 1960 never materialised and the Vincent special was subsequently sold, never to be put to test.

Early delays while Dearden concentrated on his road racing activities meant that it was a number of years before work could begin in earnest on the potential record-breaker, which in final trim emerged very much like a standard Black Lightning, with pivoting rear suspension and 'Picador' big end. With a bore and stroke 84 mm × 90 mm as the standard production Vincents, Dearden introduced many special parts including a Lucas racing magneto, a Shorrocks vane-type supercharger and a unique SU carburettor which had a bore size of $2\frac{1}{2}$ in and a massive float chamber. The bike produced an estimated 130 bhp at 6,800 rpm and had an extra long wheelbase at 64 in. It was a tragedy that all the effort and ambition never amounted to anything.

The most enduring of Vincent record-breakers was George Brown. After leaving the factory to set up his own motor cycle retail business, he raced from one record to another, first on Nero and then on the very potent, supercharged Super Nero. Missing the rides he had become used to while with Vincent, Brown picked up a burnt out (hence the name) Vincent and painstakingly he and brother Cliff built Nero into a world beater. It was repeatedly successful at almost every hill climb and sprint meeting in the country and, by 1960, had secured the world solo and sidecar kilometre standing start record. It was still very much a Vincent-based machine, though not unnaturally many non-standard parts were incorporated, including a pivoting-fork from a Velocette and a pair of AMC forks. George and Cliff Brown worked continuously on Nero, improving it over the years, and its fame spread far and wide. When the famous machine was no longer a challenge for George and Cliff Brown, they built a supercharged version and

called it Super Nero, on which George added to his growing and impressive list of national and world records. Again it was Vincent-based. On Super Nero George Brown became the fastest man in Britain on two wheels and established many sprint records, both in solo form and with a sidecar. Both Nero and Super Nero were constructed from a basic Series C Vincent frame.

Among others to distinguish themselves in speed events riding Vincent machinery were Maurice Brierley, a fine sidecar exponent with his famous 1,200 cc Methanon, and John Surtees, whose first race win was on a Vincent Grey Flash in August 1951.

It was the Grey Flash which inspired Philip Vincent to enter a team of three works riders in the 1950 Senior TT—a most courageous step, for until then no British manufacturer had dared to compete in the famous event with the regular British entries from Norton and AJS. It was, incidentally, to be another five years before another British factory had the nerve to follow Vincent's 1950 example.

The Grey Flashes were not expected to win, but they created a lot of interest and impressed by lapping suprisingly quickly at about 84 mph maximum. The machines were near-standard.

Meantime, the 1,000 cc V-twin engine was continuing to build up a formidable reputation as an efficient, extremely potent power unit, and in its Black Lightning form was getting known in motor racing circles. Cliff Brown, who built Lightnings for Ken Wharton, John Hartwell and Eric Winterbottom for their Cooper cars, still has a letter written in 1951 from a Mr. C.W. Kieft of the Kieft Car Construction Company Ltd enquiring about the possibility of having a Black Shadow engine completely stripped and rebuilt with Black Lightning components. Mr Kieft also wanted to know if Brown knew where he could get hold of one or two more Black Lightning engines since he wanted to run a team of three cars powered by the Vincent 1,000 cc engine.

A major flag-flying exercise was undertaken by Vincents in 1952 on an expedition to the famous race circuit at Montlhery, near Paris, financed by Castrol. The strategy was to attack the 24-hour record with a modified Black Shadow, and a number of other high-speed records with Gunga Din. A formidable rider-team was assembled: Phil Heath, John Surtees, Ted Davis, Robin Sherry, Johnny Hodgkin, Cyril Julian and Dennis Lashmar among them. On the first day, each rider occupying the saddle for an hour and required to exceed 100 mph during his spell of riding, the Vincent had soon captured the six-hour and 1,000-kilometre records which had been held for 17 years by Milhoux and Charlier (FN) respectively. The Black Shadow had been modified with a number of special parts including Black Lightning cams and on the hottest May day at Montlhery for years, the riders continued relentlessly in pursuit of further records. Six more records had fallen to the majestic Vincent machine when the big-ends failed after 11 hours.

Ted Davis and John Surtees attacked a number of high speed records on a Lightning the following day, but although their performance was breath-taking as they raced round the circuit at speeds of about 150 mph, they failed to secure any records. This was disappointing and almost certainly owing to the intense heat, which made it difficult to keep the tyre treads on at high speeds. Davis particularly, came close to the new short distance records, but was always thwarted as the rear tyre tread flew off before reaching the required distance. The heat also caused oiling problems, despite the use of special oils. Even so, eight new records were established to make the expedition worth while. The records, new times and previous records were as follows: 6 hours at 100.60 mph (96.72 mph); 7 hours at 99.73 mph (91.90 mph); 8 hours at 99.48 mph (91.30 mph); 9 hours at 99.40 mph (91.70 mph); 10 hours at 99.17 mph (91.54 mph); 11 hours at 92,50 mph (91.37 mph); 1,000 miles at 99.20 mph (91.36 mph); and 1,000 kilometres at 100.80 mph (96.35 mph).

Three years later, in 1955, Vincent machinery was used by speedmen on the other side of the world in New Zealand in their bid to claim an entry in the record books. Their names were Robert Burns and Russell Wright. With Black Lightning cams and a number of other modifications to his second hand Vincent Rapide, Burns added a streamlined third wheel and with little more fuss than that, exceeded the then Australian sidecar record of 122.5 mph by travelling at more than 130 mph on a local main road. It inspired him to have a crack at the outright three-wheeler record of 154 mph. To his Vincent unit he had constructed a specially designed stream-lined shell and did a practice 145 mph. He later set a new British Empire record at 145.8 mph. After a couple of months Burns was ready for his attack on

the world three-wheeler record. In the meantime colleague Russell Wright had offered him the use of his 1953 Black Lightning, which Burns had fitted with Avon Special tyres and special large port heads supplied by Philip Vincent, said to add ten mph to his performance.

December 1954 . . . and the first attempts were depressing, the engine spluttering and mis-firing, and it seemed that the attempt must fail. But after making mechanical adjustments including the fitting of new jets to the carburettors, Burns took the record at a mean 155.2 mph, against the previous record of 144 mph. Meantime, Russell Wright had set his cap at the world solo record, then standing at 180 mph. His first attempts in February 1955 were well down on the record, at 170 mph and 165 mph, but his second outward run was clocked at an impressive 192.5 mph. The world record looked a possibility as he turned for home, but when a bird crashed into the nose of the streamlining and caused Wright to drop speed, there were some anxious moments. It looked as though he had the record in the bag when he was told that the times were not correct and that he had averaged only 173 mph. Wright did not give up and in July was back on the stretch of road just outside Christchurch on which the Burns and Wright attempts were made. His first run this time was clocked at 182 mph. He was even faster on the return trip, at nearly 188 mph, and the outright world record was secure for Russell Wright and for the Vincent Lightning at almost 185 mph. In less than an hour, Burns had added the world sidecar record, again with the Vincent, at 162 mph. Russell Wright was later to try to regain his solo world record at Bonneville Salt Flats, but just failed to reach the required 200 mph.

Others who attempted to capture speed records on Vincent machinery with varied degrees of success, or failure, include the South African Vic Proctor, whose brand new unblown 1,000 cc Black Lightning crashed in a valiant attempt at the world solo record in 1950, Roy Charlton with a self-prepared 998 cc Vincent and riders like Frank Sinclair, Jack Carruthers, Les Warton and Frank Pratt.

Right *George Brown fills up Nero at Pendine, while Vic Willoughby looks almost ready to take the famous machine on test* (Motor Cycle Weekly).

Above left *George Brown and the Vincent-powered Nero flashing across Pendine Sands at 164 mph* (Motor Cycle Weekly).

Left *A Black Lightning/Watsonian racing combination at the Vincent factory in the early 1950s* (John Edwards).

Above *The Vincent drawing office in 1951. Among those in the picture are Peter West, Tony Summerville, Bob Kinolty and Assistant Chief Engineer Don Griffiths* (John Edwards).

Right *John Edwards working on modifications to the fuel injection system of the Picador V-twin timing cover* (John Edwards).

Left *The Picador engine on the brake test-bed, 45 bhp* (John Edwards).

Below left *A more light-hearted moment in the Service Department* (John Edwards).

Right *Jack Lazenby DFC (left) and mechanic Bill Bruce, in the Lightning racing shop* (John Edwards).

Below *Brian McCarthy in the Machine Service Department in 1951* (John Edwards).

Left *Sidecars ready for attaching to Vincent motor cycles* (John Edwards).

Below left *Ted Hampshire, sidecar outfit and the last Black Shadow built* (John Edwards).

Bottom left *How the final assembly section looked in the early 1950s* (John Edwards).

Above right *Ted Davis, with passenger Ernie Allen, winning the Glover Trophy at Silverstone on the Vincent/Watsonian combination in 1952* (Ted Davis).

Right *The same combination was highly successful at Brands Hatch* (Ted Davis).

BRANDS HATCH 1952

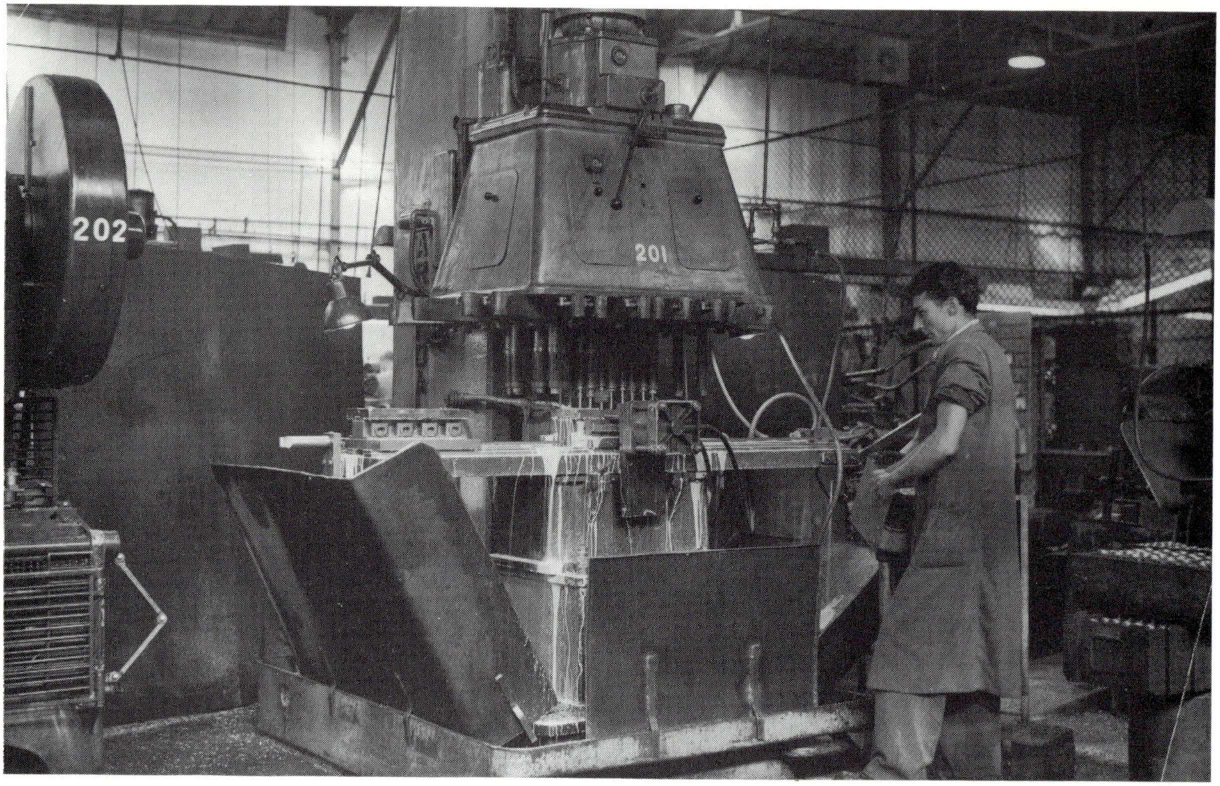
202
201

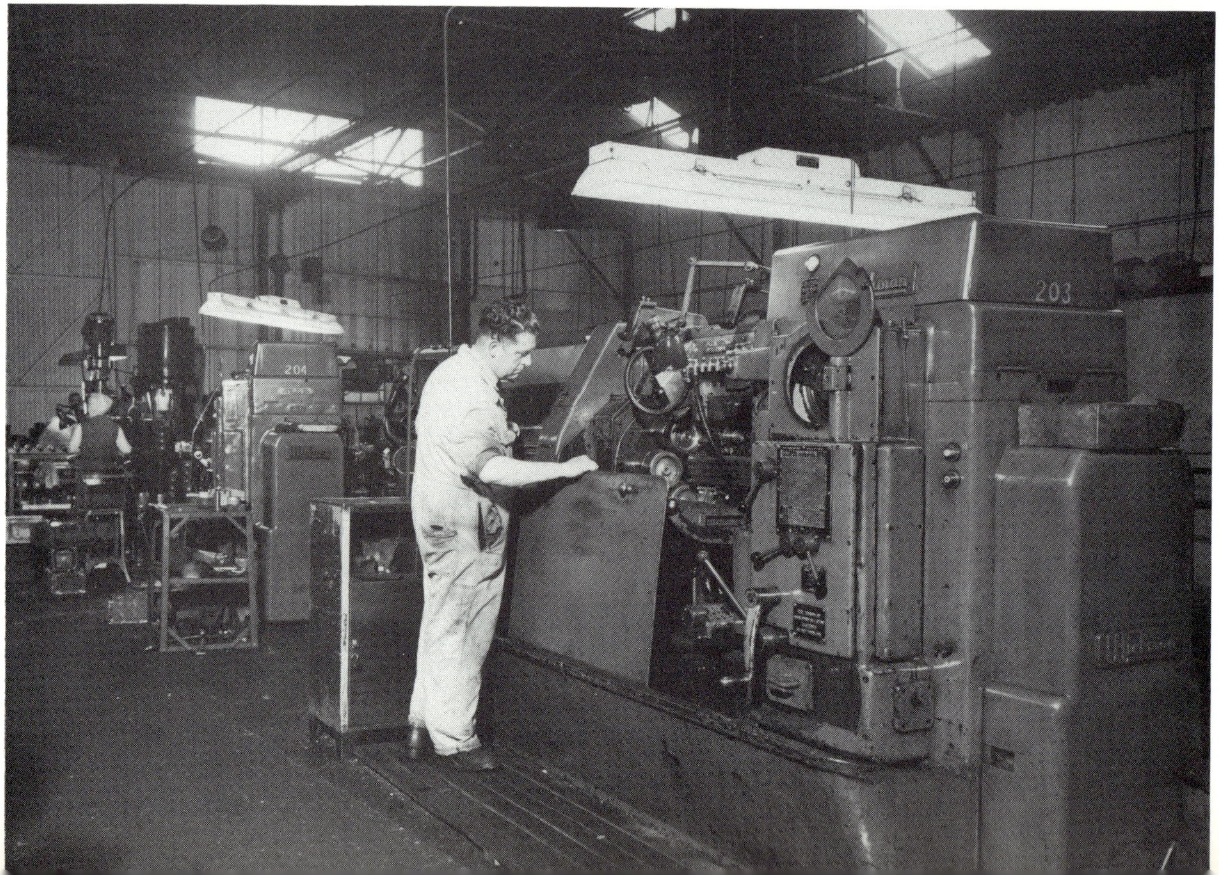
203
204

Opposite page and above *Close-ups of machinery and a general view of the Vincent Number 2 factory machine shop in the early 1950s* (Bruce).

Right *Jig borer in the Number 2 factory tool room* (Bruce).

Above left *Vincent's pit presence at Montlhery in 1952* (John Edwards). **Left** *Ted Davis (behind bike) hands over to Cyril Julian at the remarkable Montlhery record-breaking session* (Ted Davis). **Above** *The scene in the Vincent pit tells its own story of success at Montlhery. Phil Heath in riding gear* (John Edwards). **Below** *Vincent's team of selected riders, technical staff and observers at Montlhery for the record-breaking. See if you can spot John Surtees, Ted Davis, Philip Vincent, Vic Willoughby, Paul Richardson and Cyril Julian* (John Edwards).

Left *Cyril Julian on the record-breaking Black Shadow at Montlhery in 1952. Eight world records were set up by Vincent* (Ted Davis).

Below left *A 75 cc industrial engine made by Vincent in 1952 for lawnmower and other applications* (Bruce).

Above *A beautifully restored Black Shadow Series C* (Ted Davis).

Below *The outfit used by Cyril Quautrill to go on the continent* (John Edwards).

Above *Ted Davis demonstrates the acceleration of the Black Shadow in a special demonstration for* Motorcycle Sport. *It beat the Ferrari to 100 mph (Ted Davis).*

Left *Two Vincent stalwarts. Cliff Brown (with pipe) and Pat Barrett with the Vincent-powered Nero at Wellsbourn in 1953 (Cliff Brown).*

Above right *The NSU-Vincent 98 cc ohv Fox on view at the 1953 Motor Cycle Show in London (Motor Cycle Weekly).*

Right *The NSU 125 cc two-stroke Fox at the London Motor Cycle Show in 1953 (Motor Cycle Weekly).*

Left *Front end of the Fox in 1954. Note the Vincent NSU tank badge* (Motor Cycle Weekly).

Below *The NSU-Vincent 200 cc Lux of 1953* (Motor Cycle Weekly).

Right *The prototype 250 cc Max, with enclosed rear chain, narrow handlebars and a generally very handsome outline, but the cost of the German parts was prohibitive and it never went into production* (Motor Cycle Weekly).

Below right *The Firefly engine, used here to power a Hercules bicycle. It had a maximum speed of 30 mph and did 137 mpg. Vincent built 4,000 of these engines* (Ted Davis).

Above *The prototype Vincent three-wheeler photographed at the works* (Cliff Brown).

Below *A Cooper racing car powered by a 500 cc Vincent single-cylinder engine in 1954* (Ted Davis).

The dream fades

By 1954 the Vincent factory was in a critical position. It had struggled through at least two financial crises (a receiver having been appointed in 1949 who prolonged the life of the company), the three-wheeler car project had been abandoned, the profitable NSU Quickly contract was terminated and, perhaps saddest of all, while the factory had been involved in government projects like the Picador, there had been no time available to develop the Series C motor cycles.

Sales had fallen and new impetus was a desperate need. The Series D was the result, produced with great urgency. The Black Knight took over from the Rapide, the Black Prince succeeded the Black Shadow, and the new range was completed with the 500 cc Victor. They were by no means dramatically different from the earlier models, though some mechanical changes were made: improved rear suspension for instance, and coil ignition instead of a magneto. But when the Black Prince was shown for the first time at the London Motor Show of 1954, it caused a sensation, for it was fully enclosed with a sleek, glassfibre fairing painted jet black. The shock treatment was not entirely superficial, for the fairing made the machine quieter and cleaner, but the bike-buying public were not impressed. A delay of almost four months in making the new machines available to the public did nothing to stimulate sales and the factory was forced by economic necessity to bring out an unenclosed version of the Series D and this brought a welcome intake of orders. The delay was caused by supplies difficulties. Philip Vincent had become unhappy with the company with whom he had hoped to place his order for the hardened plastic required for the fairing, and was forced to search around for a new supplier.

But in any event the writing was on the wall. Philip Vincent struggled on for a while and then, in

Representing the Vincent years. Taken at the close down of motor cycle production in 1955, the picture shows Bruce Main-Smith on the latest Black Prince, Ted Davis, and Bob Brown on the pre-war Series A Rapide (Ted Davis).

September 1954, announced that continually mounting production costs on a product which would not stand a higher retail price without prejudicing sales further, had brought the company to a point where there was no financial return from the manufacture and sale of motor cycles.

For motor cycle enthusiasts it was a body blow, for Vincent was not alone in finding the situation intolerable. Only about 100 more machines were to be completed and the last Vincent motor cycle, a Black Prince, came off the production line on December 16 1955.

With motor cycle production ended, the factory turned to the manufacture of their own designed industrial engine. This had a margin of success in a small runabout water scooter and prospects appeared to brighten considerably when interest was shown by an American source. Again, it amounted to nothing, the company went into receivership yet again, and the machinery from the Stevenage works was sold off.

Among a number of people who will be forever associated with the Vincent company are Denis Minet, Ted Davis, George Buck, and of course, Phil Irving, who at the time of writing was back in Australia, but still maintaining a very close interest in all Vincent matters.

Denis Minet was a rider of some prominence and a record breaker at Brooklands. He set up the production engine assembly shop at Vincents and went on to become manager of the race shop responsible for building Lightnings and Grey Flashes.

Ted Davis joined Vincents in 1947 and left in 1959. In that time he raced both solo Vincents and sidecars, winning over 40 races with the Black Lightning sidecar outfit. He was chief development engineer when he left the company and had been closely involved with the Burns/Wright record-breaking bikes and the Series D Vincents. He now spends a lot of time restoring Vincents and writing about the famous marque in the motor cycle Press.

A most successful rider of Vincent Grey Flashes was Johnny Hodgkin, especially at Cadwell Park and in sidecar events particularly. George Buck, a well known figure at the Vincent factory, who worked in the test house, later became chief development engineer for Jaguar Cars.

Today in Stevenage the only evidence of Vincent's proud past is the impressive private house in the High Street which was PCV's home, and which is now used as offices; the original maltings which are now part of a school; and the building which Philip Vincent had built at the rear of his house as a machine shop, which is now used by the local council. The pre-war barns and shed close to the house which used to be the Vincent stores and machine, fitting, bike assembly and enamelling shops, have all been pulled down. And the building which Philip Vincent took over from the ESA company at Fishers Green in Stevenage to cope with his anticipated post-war expansion, has also been sacrificed in favour of a new factory unit which, at the beginning of 1981, was standing empty.

Before leaving Stevenage in 1960, Philip Vincent designed a new motor cycle but it was never made. Cliff Brown said of PCV: 'He was very artistic and creative and as a boss was one of the best. I always got on well with him and when I left Vincents in October 1954 he was sorry to see me go. He came into George's shop three or four times after Vincents closed down and used to say that if he had listened to some of the old hands he would still have been making motor cycles.'

He died in 1979, but there still exists a flourishing Vincent-HRD Owners' Club, there are a number of superb examples of the breed, painstakingly restored, still in existence, and a Vincent-HRD machine is a much prized and valuable possession in the 1980s.

Still at Stevenage, too, at the time of writing, are perhaps the two most famous Vincent-powered machines of all time—George Brown's Nero and Super Nero, though sadly Gunga Din was broken up years ago.

Right *The first production Black Prince in 1955* (Ted Davis).

Above *All set to go—a Vincent/Blacknell combination in 1954.*

Left *Ted Davis astride the first production Black Knight at the Vincent works in 1954 (Ted Davis).*

Above *Assembling the new Series D enclosed Vincents in 1955—roadtester George Rose and (foreground, working on machine) Alf Searle* (Ted Davis).

Right *The 1955 Series D 1,000 cc V-twin engine showing the absence of the customary down tube* (L.J.K. Setright).

Above left *1955 . . . and the last Vincent goes out on test, with Bob Brown in the riding seat. Also in the picture are Philip Vincent, E.C. Bailey (who became chairman), Ted Davis and Bruce Main-Smith (Ted Davis).*

Left *The Vincent-built Picador engine in 1958. When the project ended the engines were offered for sale (Motor Cycle Weekly).*

Above *The Vincent prototype three-wheeler with the 998 cc engine in the rear. Bruce Main-Smith is at the wheel with Ted Davis as passenger (Ted Davis).*

Right *All is revealed. The rear end of the Vincent three-wheeler of 1956 with Philip Vincent, Bruce Main-Smith and Ted Davis (Motor Cycle Weekly).*

Left *The Vincent-powered Cooper racing car (centre) in action at Mallory Park in 1956* (Ted Davis).

Below left *The Vincent factory bowls club in 1956, composed mainly of machine shop personnel* (Home Counties Newspapers).

Above right *A neat idea which never reached success—the Vincent fun water scooter* (Ted Davis).

Right *The Vincent water scooter Amanda at Frinton in 1957. Philip Vincent (centre) pulls the starter as John Bland and Ted Davis give moral support* (Ted Davis).

Left *A Vincent 998 cc being ridden round Silverstone in 1959 by C.E. Mills (Motor Cycle Weekly).*

Below *A 998 cc Vincent-powered car, now in Canada (Ted Davis).*

Right *Cliff Brown adjusting the tappets of Super Nero at Thurleigh in 1961 (Home Counties Newspapers).*

Below right *Maurice Brierley with his 1,148 cc Vincent-powered sidecar outfit, Methanon, breaking the world standing start kilometre three-wheeler record previously held by Florian Camathias at Chelveston in 1964 (British Drag Racing Association).*

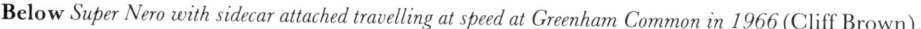

Above *One of the most famous Vincent-powered machines of all time. George Brown's 1,000 cc Super Nero supercharged sprint machine at Greenham Common in 1966* (Motor Cycle Weekly).

Below *Super Nero with sidecar attached travelling at speed at Greenham Common in 1966* (Cliff Brown).

Above *George Brown's record-breaking team: son Antony, George Brown, Mick Fraser, George Hall (timekeeper), Cliff Brown, Brian Young and Tony Driscoll* (Motor Cycle Weekly).

Below *Part of Ted Davis' impressive collection of Vincents, including a Black Lightning, Black Prince, Series B Rapide and a Series B Black Shadow* (Ted Davis).

Left *Ted Davis holds up a Firefly engine, with the Series B Shadow in the background* (Ted Davis).

Below *A restored 500 cc Vincent Grey Flash ready for action* (Ted Davis).

Right *Ted Davis judging a concours Black Shadow in 1970* (Ted Davis).

Below *Ted Davis riding a Vincent Grey Flash at Cadwell Park in 1980* (Ted Davis).

Left *Memories. Cliff Brown outside the old showroom and service department as the building looks now. Picture taken in 1980 (Cliff Brown).*

Below *Where Mr Vincent used to live . . . with, in 1980, Cliff Brown standing outside (Cliff Brown).*

Right *Reminders still in Stevenage High Street of Vincent's great days. Nero and Super Nero outside the late George Brown's shop (Cliff Brown).*

Below right *Number 2 factory at Fishers Green, Stevenage, being demolished in 1980 (Cliff Brown).*

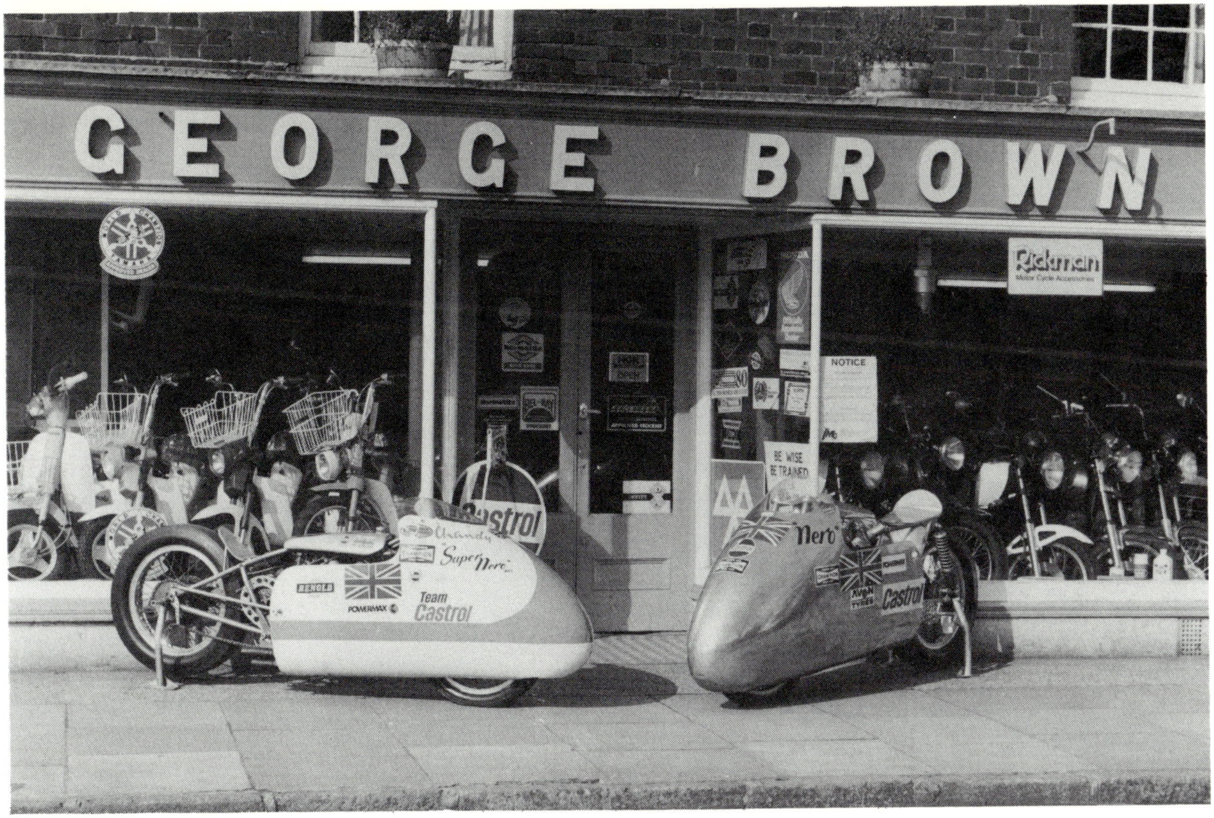
GEORGE BROWN
Rickman
NOTICE
BE WISE BE TRAINED
Castrol
Super Nero
Team Castrol
Nero
Castrol

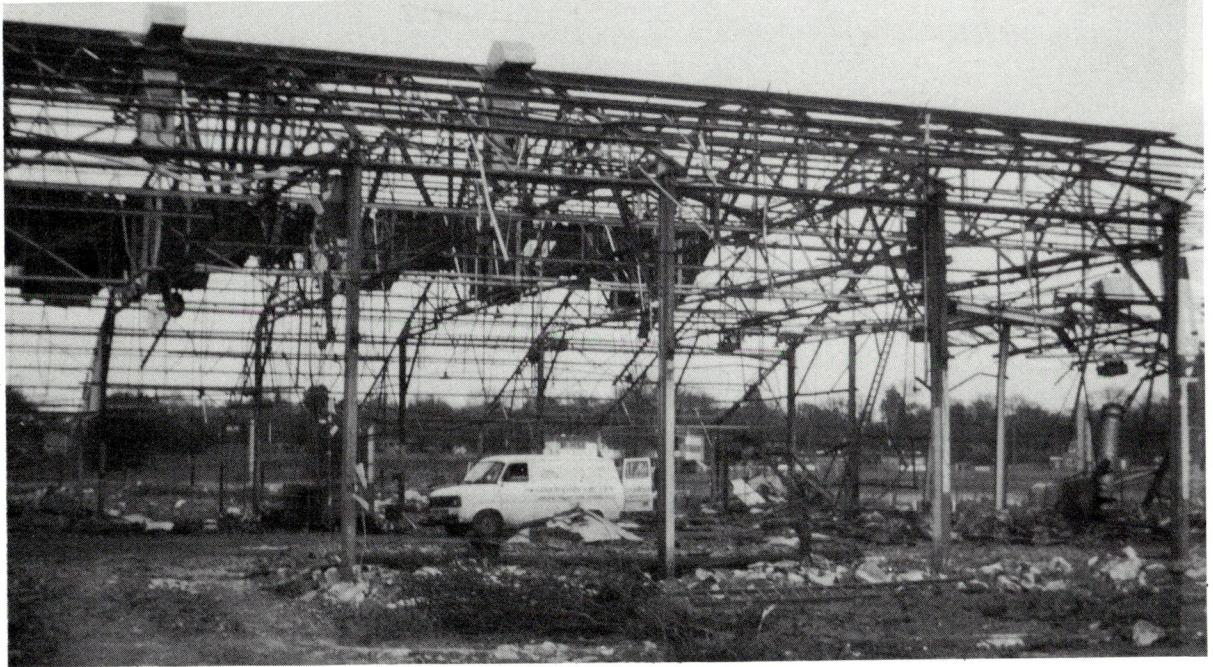

A group of 'Vincent survivors' in 1979 with Phil Irving (centre) and, extreme right, Ted Davis (Ted Davis).

The water scooter in 1957. Powered by a 200 cc engine it was capable of 20 mph (Keystone Press).